A Dog
Without Hope

A Dog Without Hope

Barby Keel
with Cathryn Kemp

SEVEN DIALS

First published in 2020 by Seven Dials,
an imprint of The Orion Publishing Group Ltd
Carmelite House, 50 Victoria Embankment,
London EC4Y 0DZ

An Hachette UK company

3 5 7 9 10 8 6 4

A CIP catalogue record for this book is
available from the British Library.

ISBN (Paperback): 978 1 409 194712
ISBN (eBook): 978 1 409 194729

Typeset by Born Group

Printed and bound in Great Britain by Clays Ltd, Elcograf S.p.A.

www.orionbooks.co.uk

To my father, who was the heart and soul of the sanctuary. May he rest in peace. I'll meet you again on Rainbow Bridge.
Love, Barby xx

CONTENTS

Introduction

Over the years, I have fostered thousands of animals, including hundreds of dogs. Many arrive at the door of the Barby Keel Animal Sanctuary in a terrible state; beaten, neglected or abandoned by the humans who were meant to care for them. Some, like little pup Prince, come with terrible problems, some deliberately caused by their owners, some the result of unthinking neglect or dire poverty. Some are simply left because they are not wanted any more, or abandoned because of a change in their owner's life circumstances.

Whatever the reason for the dog reaching my sanctuary, each canine that I take in is given a warm bed, whatever medical care they might require and the support they will invariably need to recover, if they can.

To us, each dog represents a little life, a precious creature, a soul as important as that of any human.

It is my life's mission to give any animal that appears at my door a safe place to stay, food for their tummies and the love and attention they may never have received before.

I am fortunate that I don't have to do this alone, and, actually, it would be impossible. I have a team of dedicated volunteers and staff, which, as anyone who knows me, is well aware I call my 'motley crew'. They come from all walks of life, from the richest to the poorest, and everyone in between. What unites us, what drives us each and every day, is our desire to look after those animals that literally have no one, and nowhere else in this world to call home.

I didn't set out to create my private sanctuary. Mine is only one of a handful operating in this country, and there's a very good reason for this. Running an animal sanctuary, especially one like ours, which has a no-destroy policy except in cases of extreme pain or terminal illness, is extremely expensive, takes relentless hard work, and, at times, can feel utterly thankless. I would go as far as to say that it is a ridiculous thing to do. No right-minded person would ever attempt it.

However, when it comes to animals, I've never been in my right mind. My father, who died aged ninety-six after a lifetime of taking in strays and unwanted creatures, taught me how to love through his passion for animals. I inherited that passion.

I would sit on his knee as a child and drop milk into a tiny bird's beak as he held it so very gently. He would have found the hatchling in a hedgerow perhaps, abandoned by its mother who may have fallen foul of a local cat. He would bring it home, trembling in his hands, which were red and scarred from working as a chef in a hotel kitchen. He was so caring, so doting towards any beast, big or small, scaly or fluffy, exotic or domesticated, that I couldn't help but carry on his legacy as I grew up.

I don't think either Dad or myself could've imagined where that legacy would take me. More than thirty years later, I have a menagerie of animals under my protection: from geese to hens, pigs to goats and sheep, wild horses to donkeys, peacocks, bushbabies, mice, ducks, dogs, rabbits, guinea pigs and hundreds of cats.

It didn't start this way; I didn't ever set out to create what I have today. You have to give up everything else, devote your life to the creatures you care for. You have to find ever larger sums of money to be able to care for them, and to what end? Only the knowledge that you are doing something *right*, something noble even. Every now and then I am given awards and trophies for the work I do, and while I appreciate the recognition and the sensibility behind those awards, they aren't the reason I do it.

When I was old enough to work and save money, I decided to buy land in Sussex. My idea was to keep a few horses, perhaps have lots of dogs, but I never for one moment thought of starting an animal rescue shelter. Who would be foolish enough to do such a thing?

From the moment I stepped out of my battered old car and put my foot onto the soil that still lies under my feet, I knew I was home. I bought this land, a few acres in the countryside, with the help of Les, my partner at the time, in 1971. I had saved for years from money I'd earned from working as a waitress in the seaside town of Eastbourne, where I originate from.

At first, Les and I lived in a large prefabricated house that we built ourselves. It looked rather like one of the prefabs built to create quick housing after the Second World War. We put it together, piece by piece, making sure we had a large wood burner in the centre to make it cosy. Outside, the land was open and free with barely a hedge or stile to contain the fields or animals that first lived there.

Over time that changed. I already had four animals: Zede, an Alsatian, Pip, my spaniel and Dene, a bushbaby that my father had 'rescued' from a shabby local pet shop, the kind that thankfully don't exist any more. Within a week I had been given a horse that a friend couldn't afford to keep any more, a donkey that had been abandoned in a field and left to die, and several goats, which arrived in mysterious circumstances. I had gone out to feed the horse and donkey one fine autumn morning, and was stunned to find them tethered to my old wooden gatepost. I would never have dreamed of turning the goats away. I led them into the wide-open fields and set them free, letting them roam wild as they were meant to, across my land. Those first few creatures were the trickle that became a flood.

Within weeks, my reputation for taking in animals started to spread like wildfire. Word got out as the gossip-mongers, the chattering neighbours, the interested parties such as the vets and my friends, all shared the news: Barby will take in any animal, regardless of its condition or background.

Well, that was that. What started as a few waifs and strays became a steady stream of stray cats, abandoned dogs, unwanted puppies, horses, sick rabbits and alongside them a cacophony of geese, ducks, goats and sheep, and I couldn't refuse them the dignity of sharing my land. In those days, I had only the boundary fence around my eight-acre fringes to keep them contained. They were free, and so was I.

Nothing has really changed in the fifty years since I set up home here on the outskirts of Bexhill-on-Sea, except that I have many more miles of fencing now, and pens, hutches, crates and kennels to separate the six hundred or so animals who live here. Our boundaries contain some of the saddest, most heartbreaking stories of neglect and abuse inflicted upon the beasts that live here, and yet it is a place of hope, a place of sanctuary and safety. This is a special place, a view shared by everyone who works here.

It is a place of ordinary and extraordinary miracles, where animals come to be healed and to heal those who care for them in turn. I watch the relationships between my crew and the creatures, and I can never be sure who is helped most by the care given and the love received.

I became an animal fosterer because of this symbiotic relationship, this shared experience of loving care, this self-less rescuing of otherwise unwanted animals, and perhaps unwanted humans too. It never ceases to surprise and delight me.

This life is an emotional rollercoaster, though. Animals sicken. They can be so badly hurt that they don't survive our ministrations. The people who care for them have their own struggles, their own issues to contend with too, yet despite all that, I truly believe that it is the best job in the world.

My hope is that every living creature can find a place of safety and sanctuary, and those that come to my door will always have a home, and will live out their lives with dignity at the Barby Keel Animal Sanctuary.

ONE

Neglect

The sticky vinyl tiles felt cold and hard under my tummy as I lay on the kitchen floor. I had never had a proper bed and so I was left to make do, sleeping where I could, trying not to think about how uncomfortable I felt. My tail was tucked between my legs and my ears were back. I could hear footsteps and I shivered, wondering if they would come in my direction.

As the sound got closer, I pricked up my little ears and jumped up onto my four legs, quaking a little in fright. I had no idea what mood my owner would be in, or if it was indeed him or one of his friends, though none of them paid me much attention either.

I looked up as the door handle turned, and jumped up, giddy with excitement. Perhaps this time my owner would come in and speak to me kindly? Perhaps this time he would tickle me under the chin or stroke my small ears and tell me what a good puppy I was? Perhaps he might even pick me up and hold me close so I could feel a warm body next to me and feel the same comfort I used to feel snuggled up with my brothers and sisters against my mummy's belly? Hope reared up in me, and small though I was, I started to bark with all my power, my voice echoing in the largely unfurnished space.

There were no sofas here, no cushions or blankets to curl up on, just the cold vinyl floor, a metal table and wooden chairs shoved next to a bare wall and a freestanding cooker. The dust on the floor made my nose tickle, and I could smell the lingering scent of long-since eaten food from the overflowing rubbish bin in one corner.

Just as I was certain the person on the other side would turn away from the door, making me lie back down with a long sigh, it finally opened. I tried to scramble up, whining a little as my tummy felt sore from hunger, hoping that this time whoever it was would remember to feed me. My paws slipped on the vinyl, making me scrabble up in an undignified way. I looked up. The man, who seemed to me to be impossibly tall, towered over me.

Relief replaced uncertainty. It was my master!

I leapt up to him, my tiny tail wagging. My tummy was rumbling but at that moment I was too excited to care. He looked down at me. He was a tall man with hair shaved close to his head and arms marked with black drawings. Held between his lips was a long white stick that was on fire. The smell made my stomach jolt and I felt sick suddenly.

Despite this, I wagged my tail as hard as I could and whined a little, my happiness at the prospect of a meal or even an affectionate stroke too much to contain.

He stood there for a moment and seemed to sway slightly. Confused, I sat down abruptly and peered up at him. He looked down at me but didn't seem to see me. His eyes were glassy and there was another strong smell coming off him, the scent that came with the cans he drank from.

I whined again, which brought him to his senses, a little at least.

'What did I want? Oh yes, I remember . . .' His voice was strange. He slurred his words but he seemed to refocus. His gaze left mine and clutching the top of one of the chairs, he stumbled over to a cupboard and reached inside, taking out more of the shiny metal cans of the liquid he always drank.

I tried again to get his attention, running in circles around his legs as he walked. He moved forwards and in doing so, trod on my tail. A bolt of pain seared through me. I yelped loudly, a high-pitched squeak, which made my master shout.

'Bloody animal! Why are you always under my feet? Get away from me, or you'll get worse.'

Even his anger was slurred. Instantly, I froze.

I had been bounding up and down, trying to run around his legs, to show him how happy I was to see him, to try and tell him how very hungry I was and how thirsty too, but he couldn't, or wouldn't, listen to me.

His voice was loud, louder still when he shouted at me with words I didn't understand. Nonetheless, the intended meaning was clear as daylight.

His face leered into mine. And I began to tremble harder, my short fur standing up, my long tail firmly between my legs. My ears were fully back as I waited for what would come next.

His face came closer to mine. I dropped my eyes down to the floor and put my head on my paws, still waiting for his reaction. I had caught a glimpse of his face. It was red and blotchy, screwed up with rage. His chin was dark with stubble and he smelled unwashed.

'Stay there,' he sneered at last, 'or you'll get this.' He showed me his fist curled up in a ball. I whimpered with fright, not knowing what he was going to do.

I tried to back even further into my corner but there was no room to be had; nowhere to go. I started to cry. I was scared, hungry and thirsty, and by now I knew that neither a meal nor a drink would be coming for me. I had upset this giant of a man who forgot to pet me, who shouted at me and said nasty things. I whimpered again, my little heart breaking at the thought that I would be left in this horrible place, cold and frightened, and worst of all, so terribly alone.

My life hadn't started this way. In the beginning, I was surrounded by squirming, snuffling brothers and sisters, each of us crawling over the other and clinging to the warm, comforting body of our mother. She would lick us to keep us clean, her big tongue almost knocking me sideways as she worked. I was surrounded by familiar smells, the taste of my mummy's milk and all the wriggling warm bodies that made me feel so safe and protected.

But one day, before I could walk properly on my large paws and long spindly legs, a man, the man who became my owner, came to visit. He picked up a few of my siblings, and then it was my turn. He held me up, my legs dangling down, and I licked his face to see if he was worth loving. The taste of him was strange, sweat mixed with the funny taste of those long white sticks that had fire at the ends of them. I didn't like it and I struggled to get free.

Even though I was trying to get away, something about the sight of me struggling made the man laugh. I looked at him, quizzically, and was relieved when he placed me back into the safety and security of my mother's large dog bed.

'Oh look, she likes you!' came the voice of the nice lady who looked after my mother. I looked over at her and gave her a short bark and wagged my tail.

'Oh how sweet, she's agreeing,' she laughed.

I had no idea what they were saying and quickly lost interest in the man once I was back with my family. Soon I was rolling on the floor, barking playfully as one of my brothers tried to chew my ear.

Some time passed, I don't know how much, and the man reappeared. I had just finished wolfing down a plate of puppy food and was feeling a little sleepy, when he stood over me, and with big arms covered in dark patterns, he reached down for me.

I didn't have time to object. I was held aloft again, though this time I didn't lick his nose. I wrinkled up my nose and used my growing strength to wriggle free of his grasp again.

'This one,' was all the man said. I didn't understand him, but the lady who looked after us came over to me, stroked my ears the way I liked, then snapped the leash onto my collar.

That could only mean a walk. I jumped up at her in excitement.

'Get down you naughty thing,' she said kindly. 'She's excited to go out, thinking it must be w.a.l.k.i.e.s . . .' she added, spelling out a word that made the man's stern face break out in a grin. He looked like he didn't smile very often, and the effect on his face was odd.

I stopped bouncing, suddenly uncertain – this wasn't the time I usually went out for walkies. Up until now, we'd had a routine set in stone. Walkies first thing, then breakfast, then a day spent playing and dozing before dinner then a last walk before bed. The change made me feel suddenly unsettled. I looked over at the kind lady and wagged my tail a little to try and gauge her reaction.

She didn't meet my eyes. Instead she bent over and tickled me under the chin, saying, 'She's a lovely dog, we're really going to miss her.' She sounded momentarily sad, and I looked up at her quizzically, but she quickly broke into a grin, so I decided everything must be fine.

Then she handed the man the end of my lead. I cocked my head sideways, staring at her, but the urge to go outside and run overcame my curiosity. My tail started to wag, I got up and as soon as the man started to walk out of the back door, I leapt out joyfully.

'She still needs lots of training on the lead; she's a very happy puppy but her enthusiasm for walks overcomes her. You'll need to work on that, I'm afraid.'

The lady was waving from the door. I turned around, really puzzled now. Why did she look like she was saying goodbye?

'I'll sort her out, don't worry. Come on, dog – into the car.' He spoke gruffly. As he said the words, he opened the boot of his car and gestured for me to get into it. In the back was a dog crate, the kind we slept in overnight. I stood there, looking at him, unsure what to do. I didn't want to get inside that car. It didn't smell right, there were no other dogs in there and my family was still inside. Surely, we should all go together?

'Come on, get into the car. Do as I say, dog.' His voice was strict now and his smile was replaced by a frown that creased his pale skin.

Still, I didn't budge. I didn't like him and I didn't like the thought of getting into his car.

All of a sudden, he swooped down, picked me up and half threw me into the crate. The shock of his swift movement made me compliant, and so I stayed there, at the back of the crate, looking at him as he closed it and slammed the boot shut. It made a terrible noise, and I felt frightened. I didn't move, my long legs trembling underneath me in fear.

At least something smelled of home. There was a blanket in the crate that had come from the nice lady's house as I could smell her scent and that of the house upon it. The man got into the driver's seat and shut his door with another loud bang. I whimpered this time.

'Shut up, dog, you belong to me now.' The man spoke abruptly as the car moved off, winding slowly down the country lane that led away from my home. As the car heaved from side to side, I slumped onto the blanket, my paws tucked under my chin, and watched in silence as the countryside turned to concrete, as the fields and hedges turned to houses and street lamps. I had never been this far from home and I wondered when he would take me back. I wanted a nap next to my mother. I wanted to hear her long-contented sigh as we all settled down next to her to sleep. I started to miss her, and I wanted to go home. I knew I had to tell the man that he'd gone the wrong way and we needed to go home now. The only way I knew to say it was to bark and so I barked and barked. I got louder and louder, but the man didn't understand me. He started to shout at me.

'STOP BLOODY BARKING!' His voice sounded angry and I immediately stopped. I didn't want him to be cross with me, I just wanted to go home to my family.

The journey seemed endless. We were in the car for a long time, and I hated the movement as we bumped along the uneven roads. I lay down, my head on my paws, feeling sick and frightened. Where was I going? What was happening to me?

After what seemed like forever, the car stopped. The man got out and within seconds the boot was opened. I sniffed the air. It smelled very different to home. Gone were the scents of foxes and cats, the small creatures that made my whole body bristle with excitement. Gone were the sweet-smelling grasses and hedgerows, the plants and insects buzzing around them. They had been replaced by exhaust fumes, people with those white sticks in their mouths, beeping horns and the noise of traffic, which made my head hurt even though we'd only just arrived. But arrived where?

'Out. Come on, out, we're home.'

I looked at the man. Something was dawning on me, a thought I didn't much like at all. Perhaps this was where I was going to live now. Perhaps he'd taken me away from my family forever.

The thought made me cry. I started to howl, my whole body shaking as I lamented my lost family.

The man muttered something under his breath and he reached in and grabbed me, hurting my tummy as he roughly pulled me out.

'When I tell you to come, I expect you do it now,' he said, speaking louder this time. I didn't know what he was saying to me but it sounded unpleasant, which made me cry all the harder.

The man fumbled with his keys at the door, and soon I was carried in along a small corridor that smelled of food and the smoke from the sticks. He placed me down with more care than he'd done so far in a small room. I looked around, recognising nothing, smelling nothing that was familiar, wondering why on earth I was there, so far away from my mother.

A moment later, the crate appeared, along with the blanket, bringing with it some feeling of security with its familiar smell. I crawled inside the crate, whimpering as I went, feeling thoroughly confused, my tummy starting to grumble and my head hurting.

At first the man was kind enough to me. After I'd got over my shock, I got used to the new smells, the few rooms and the cartons of food left on the floors. I was fed, if not always twice a day, at least once a day, and he took me out for a few walks, though not every day. During those first few days, I walked around, searching in every nook and cranny, looking for my siblings everywhere, trying to sniff them out, calling to them, until, at last, I realised they were gone. I was alone here in this strange place with a growing hole of sadness in my heart.

TWO

Horror Crash

Every day was the same. Every day I felt hungry and thirsty. Every day I was left alone for most of the time in that same dismally small kitchen. My blanket, the only thing I had to comfort me with memories of my life before when I snuggled down at night, had been taken away after I messed inside.

That day, he'd forgotten to take me for my morning walk. I'd waited by the door for hours, occasionally wagging my tail at the slightest sound coming from beyond it. My tummy rumbled as I hadn't been fed since early the previous day, and I was becoming desperate to relieve myself. Time dragged past and still he didn't come.

It was the only real routine we had: each morning he'd feed me then take me out for a walk down the tarmac roads, weaving across busy roads with terrifying large cars and lorries rumbling past. The joy at being taken from that room managed to overpower the fear I felt from all the noise, and I kept going, bouncing alongside my owner, sniffing at each lamppost, revelling in the smells of the dogs and cats that left their scent, marking the territory in the streets around my master's home. Then we'd return home, and I'd stop bouncing and walk as slowly as I could back into that room where I knew I would be left for hours, ignored and abandoned as the television blared from the next room and my sobs were stifled by the noise.

When finally, I heard his footsteps on the day I messed on my blanket, it was late afternoon, and I had backed into the darkest corner of the room by the mop and bucket, knowing I would be in trouble.

I had been trained by the nice lady, the memory of whom was fading fast, to go outside when I was on my walks, and I knew I was now a bad puppy. I'd done the unthinkable and messed where I slept.

His face showed his reaction immediately. 'What's that stink?' he yelled. 'You bloody dog, what the hell have you done now?'

His voice was loud and hurt my small ears. It scared me and I began to tremble all over. I tried to back further into the dark space but there was nowhere to hide from his wrath.

'Bloody hell, look what I've got to clear up now, what a way to start the day.'

I whimpered and tried to wag my tail as if to say, 'Please forgive me.'

My actions were in vain. If anything, they made my owner angrier. He slammed the door shut, making me jump with fright, banged the cupboards as he looked for something to clean it up and swore to himself as he worked.

I started to whine and to wag my tail harder. I was desperate for a gentle touch, a soft stroke, a tickle under my chin, anything that might give me some affection or comfort to make it all alright. Nothing came, of course. I knew he was in no mood to stroke me but every part of me yearned for a kind word or gesture to take the nasty feelings away.

'Right, I'd better take you out, come on, NOW!'

My head down, I trotted after him. As he left, he suddenly turned and grabbed the blanket, the one that still smelled faintly of my owner, the woman who gave me strokes and told me I was a beautiful girl.

'And this, this goes from today. You don't deserve it, you little monster.' I looked up at him. His face was ugly, creased up with anger, and he was holding my blanket up and shaking it at me. I cocked my head to the side as if to say, 'What now? What are you doing?'

At the sight of me he seemed to lose his temper completely. He was incandescent with rage. He put his face close to mine, making me jump up and bark in shock, then he said, with a sneer, 'You won't ever sleep on this again, filthy animal.'

He marched over to the rubbish bin and stuffed the blanket inside. I still had no idea what he was doing. I barked, standing stiff on all fours, feeling like I had to defend myself though I was still only a puppy.

'I wish I'd never got you. I'm taking you out for a walk now.'

I hesitated. Despite the anger in his voice, I wanted a walk more than anything.

He reached for the lead, and my instincts took over. I bounded over to him, suddenly happy again, my tail wagging furiously and letting out little yelps of joy. At last, we could go outside; at last, I could leave this horrible kitchen; for a little while, at least.

However hard I tried on that day, or thereafter, it was clear that after messing inside, I had lost whatever small love he'd ever felt for me. I knew that I was a bad dog, and I could never redeem myself in his eyes. He showed it with every word, action and deed. He barely touched me unless his hand accidentally brushed my nose as he put down my morning bowl of food. He barely acknowledged me, leaving me alone for hours on end, with nothing to play with, no human comfort or relief at all. I slept on the cold floor as my crate had been taken away too, sighing with sadness as I settled down alone each night. I got more and more bored as I grew bigger, and started to chew the chairs and bark at the table legs. I desperately needed some companionship and stimulation, neither of which I received.

Each morning when he walked in in his dirty dressing gown, I ran up to him hoping that *this* would be the day he would notice me properly, would say something nice, would reach down and pat me on the head. It never happened. Each day I went to sleep with my belly rumbling and my soul almost crushed with the pain of being so unwanted.

The smell hit me first, wafting through the open door. The enticing scent of sausages cooking made my mouth water with great strings of dribble that sank slowly to the floor. It was the first time my owner had ever failed to shut me in to the kitchen, and I stared in confusion at the gap leading out from my prison.

I edged out of the kitchen, wide-eyed with fear, terrified that by straying beyond the boundaries of the kitchen I was being a bad puppy again. My hunger led me onwards, though, a sensation of gnawing emptiness in my tummy that overcame every impulse to stay inside and be a good dog.

I don't know why he had left the door open, but there had been lots of noises overnight, and I'd been kept awake all night by people laughing raucously in the lounge and by the strong smell of smoke.

The next morning I awoke, and found, to my surprise and delight, that the door was wide open. I blinked, then leapt up, sniffing at the air, still heavy with smoke but with something else, something wonderful. I followed my nose out of that room and into the small hallway.

Then, the most amazing discovery of all. The front door, the place beyond which was the outdoors, had been left ajar. I hardly knew whether to run over or hesitate, checking whether I was allowed. Had my master left it open deliberately? Then the smell of sausages cooking wafted over again and the decision was made in an instant.

It didn't take me a moment to race over and scrabble at it, opening the door wider inch by inch, forcing my nose through it and, with a last look behind me to check I wasn't being watched, I made my way outside.

For a moment, the sensations of the road and streets overwhelmed me, and I stood still, taking it all in. A truck hooted its horn, a car zoomed past, a man yelled at someone, while nearby, a few teenagers kicked stones in a bored kind of way. The smells and sights outside always proved such a sharp contrast to my kitchen home that I usually was overcome for the first few minutes, adjusting to the change in pace, the noises that battered my small ears, the feel of the concrete under my tender paws, which, though I was growing fast, were still too large for my legs.

But today was different. Today, the most tantalising smell had emboldened me, was drawing me outside further and further away from the safety of my master's flat.

My belly was empty. I hadn't been fed for almost twenty-four hours. The need for food took over completely. I stood there, rigid for a moment, letting the scent of meat cooking settle into my nostrils, then I leapt forwards, racing over to the hot dog stall that had set up across the road.

The scent was overpowering. I ran, my paws flailing, my tail revolving like a helicopter, my heart pounding as I crossed the pavement and flew into the road towards that beautiful, tempting smell of food. I was drooling in readiness; my stomach was growling. There was nothing in my mind except the thought of sinking my jaws into the meat, then I heard a bang, like the loudest thunder I'd ever heard. There was a crash, a sensation of flying and then nothing.

I didn't feel the impact. I heard a crunch, then a cry but whose it was I didn't know. There was a squeal of tyres, lights flashed, then everything went black.

Everything hurt. I felt sick. My head felt woozy. Shapes appeared around me, then everything went black again. Then there was pain, so much pain. I cried and cried, my leg was hurting, then nothing again. Gentle hands held me. Voices over my head stirred me and I looked around. I was in a clean, white room with a bright light over my head. A man wearing a green mask stood over me. His eyes were kind, someone stroked my ears then held me down. I didn't struggle. I had no fight in me. I couldn't move, I didn't understand anything, except for the kindness I was being shown. I felt a sharp prick, then, in seconds, the room and all the people and things in it disappeared.

Waking up hours later, I felt strange, so very strange. Something wasn't right. I tried to scrabble up, but I couldn't move. The nausea returned and I lay my head back down, exhausted by this small effort.

I peered up again. What was wrong? Why did everything feel different? Then I saw it, the thing that was wrong. Where my front leg was, was now just a stump. I tried to struggle again but the effort proved too much and I sank back down, a whimper rising in my throat, a sob that would fill me up to bursting.

I lay down, not understanding, not knowing what had happened. I thought fleetingly of my owner, but instead of the man, I remembered my mistress, her look of love as she tickled my tummy when I was very small. With her lovely smiling face in my mind, I sank back into unconsciousness.

THREE

Dumped

The large female pig had arrived from a deserted farm only days earlier. She was a handsome beast, with a huge snout, pale pink skin dotted with large black spots and she wolfed down her meals with a zest we all enjoyed watching.

I'd come down to the pen early, intending to hang about and watch the pig as she fed, probably giving her a little scratch on the snout or a stroke of her hairy back, but to my surprise, she hadn't come to meet me, as she had done each morning since she'd arrived.

Concerned that something was wrong, I climbed over the fence, stepping onto the sweet-smelling hay, marvelling at the cleanliness of this most fastidious animal, and poked my head into the gloom of her pen, which consisted of a wooden structure with slats for walls and a roof, and plenty of straw, beneath which she appeared almost buried.

It was a late summer day and the sun was already up, though it was only six-thirty. The sky looked heavy, with dark grey clouds hanging ominously overhead, and it was humid. It felt like a storm was brewing, and already the sky had a yellowish hue and the sharp tang of rain. The light seemed to sharpen the scents of the site too. On my walk down, I had breathed in the smell of soil, grass, and the rich scent of the animals of all shapes and sizes who lived in this special place.

'Come on, girl, poke your head out and say hello. Are you poorly, madam?' I enquired, stretching my neck a little further into the space.

A snort greeted me, which I took to be a good sign, and I crept further in, not wanting to disturb her sleeping area, which I knew she would've spent time arranging as she liked it, as pigs do. Pigs never soil in their sleeping quarters, and instead it smelled of dry grass, summer and something else, something earthy.

'Where are you? Come out, girl, it's time for breakfast.'

Then I saw what was stopping her. The pig, who we'd christened Dolly, was laid out in the furthest end of the shack, and lined up, gulping down their fill of milk, were five newborn piglets.

'Oh, you clever girl!' I exclaimed. 'We didn't even know you were expecting babies! Oh, you beauty!'

I stood there for a moment, awestruck by the simplicity of nature, and the wonder of seeing new life appear as if by magic. Whether it was the lambs being born each spring, the mares giving birth to their foals, or a litter of new kittens squirming and mewing for their mother, there was something marvellous, something miraculous, about each new creature entering the world, a sense of newness and beginning that never failed to move me profoundly.

I stood there, staring at them, for what seemed like hours though it was probably only a few minutes, when I heard the sound of a squeaky wheelbarrow wheel and knew that Dan, my farm manager, was nearby. I couldn't wait to tell him.

'Come this way, I've got a surprise for you, you great oaf,' I called out to him good-naturedly.

'What is it, I haven't got all day. You're such a slave-driver, I've got enough to do without stopping to talk to you,' he sighed, though I knew he was only teasing.

Dan was a young man who stood over six foot tall, towering over my diminutive frame of barely five foot. He had dark curly hair that he wore long, and round glasses. He always wore a ragged old T-shirt, a pair of wellies that had seen better days, and a pair of jeans so ripped that part of one leg was almost hanging off. He had a huge grin on his face.

'Stop moaning and come and look at this,' I said proudly as I moved away from the entrance to the pen.

Dan peered inside, then I heard his gasp.

'We didn't know she was pregnant, did we?' he said, poking his head back out.

I shook my head in response. We were both grinning goofily, both touched by the extraordinary magic of birth.

'We'll have to build more pens,' Dan grumbled, though he was still smiling.

'We will,' I agreed, 'and I know just the man to do it . . .'

'Five piglets, what a good girl,' Dan sighed.

'Didn't she do well. And with no one to help her! She just got on with it. It's no wonder she was eating so much!' I laughed.

Dan chuckled. 'Well, I'd better get on. Thanks for showing me, Barby. When I've fixed this blasted barrow, I'll have a think about where we can get more building supplies from.' Dan looked at me pointedly and indicated the barrow, which was trailing feed behind him due to a rusted hole in one side.

My brow creased with worry. We were badly in need of funds. Our latest vet bill had come in and ran into thousands of pounds, just for one month. Our equipment was starting to break and we urgently needed more land to expand the menagerie. Every day animals arrived, and as fast as we tried to rehome the ones we were able to, more still came. On just one day that week, we'd had six cats, one dog and several other animals of various species all arrive on our doorstep. We were running out of space, and money. Funds were a constant source of worry to me. As a private sanctuary, we received no public money and had only just converted to charity status. We relied on donations from the many people, both local and nationwide, who knew about our work and gave generously at the many coffee mornings, bring-and-buy sales, summer and Christmas fairs, and, of course, those who so kindly left us legacies in their wills.

Running this place sometimes felt like an endless uphill struggle, with more and more animals to care for each year and the accompanying increase in expenditure entailed.

'I'll put an ad in the local paper asking for second-hand garden equipment. Someone out there might be able to help.' I shrugged. Right then, it was all I could do.

Just then, a distant rumble of thunder reverberated across the valley. I looked up and felt the first, fat droplets of rain as they started to fall from the inky-grey sky.

'Watch out, there's a storm coming,' I said, holding my face up to the heavens, welcoming the feeling amid the haze of humidity.

'Go on, Harry, go back inside the house. To your bed!' I commanded to the dog waiting patiently by my side. Harry, a large spaniel, was a rescue dog that had been with me for a few years. He was a handsome chap, with thick, light-coloured fur, long floppy ears and eyes as black as coal. When he'd arrived, he'd had a volatile temper and had bitten several of the volunteers. As he was a large, well-built dog this obviously caused some chaos, and it was the reason he had never been rehomed. I had no idea why he'd started biting, but my best guess was that he'd been severely mistreated and left to run amok. It took many months of patient training, walking him up and down the yard on a leash, giving him treats every time he passed a chicken without attempting to bite or eat it, to help shape him into the gentle dog he was today.

He never attempted to bite anyone any more but he'd retained a streak of naughtiness. I knew I would have to keep Harry. I could never have trusted him enough to send him off to a foster home, and over time I'd grown to love his wilful ways. He still tried to chase the chickens occasionally, but he knew I wouldn't stand for anything worse than that.

He was perpetually grumpy, though, and would often sulk, or go off for hours in a mood, which I found amusing rather than exasperating. Each dog has its own distinct personality, and I loved them all, even if my Harry had the devil in him!

Harry needed little encouragement to go inside and ran for shelter as the rain got heavier. A streak of lightning lit up the field and the thunder sounded again, this time louder.

The animals, which had been fidgety and restless overnight, sensing the oncoming change in the weather, started to bleat and snort, cluck and bark as the skies opened, unleashing a summer rainstorm that took my breath away.

'Get inside, Barby, we don't want you to be struck by lightning!' Dan laughed, shouting at me over the noise of the rain.

'Oh yeah, right, I bet you'd love that!' I shouted back, looking over towards the sanctuary entrance, wondering whether I would make it before the next roll of thunder. Since I was a girl, and caught up in the bombing raids on Eastbourne in the Second World War, I have never liked loud bangs or storms, as they remind me too much of that terrible time, crouched in a dripping wet, dark shelter, hearing the vibration of the Luftwaffe overhead and the crashing as bombs fell, not knowing if we would survive the night.

The heavens lit up again, and at that moment, I saw something move by the front gate. I squinted over, the flash from the lightning disappearing as fast as it had come, leaving me looking through a heavy sheet of rain at a black shape. The shape of a person, I was sure of it.

'There's someone at the gate,' I shouted to Dan.

No sooner had the words left my mouth than the sanctuary bell rang, its familiar clanging noise cutting through the downpour and drowning out my voice.

'I have to go and see who's there. An animal may be in trouble,' I shouted. This time Dan heard me.

'Stay here, Barby, I'll go, you'll get soaking wet.'

Our attention was completely diverted from the snug little piglets, all scrambling over their mother's belly, sucking at her for milk. Dolly looked up at us, as if to ask 'What's going on?' but then grunted and settled her head back down again, safe in the comfort of her pen. She must've been exhausted from the birth and too preoccupied with her babies to worry about the storm coming.

'No, I'll go. I don't mind a soaking. You stay here and make sure Dolly is alright.' With that, I pulled my T-shirt up over my head and made a mad dash for the sanctuary entrance.

As I ran, I nearly slipped over several times on the concrete yard, which was smeared with soil, straw and the droppings from our resident ducks, geese and chickens.

'I'm coming. Don't leave,' I yelled, waving at the person who was standing there. I hoped and prayed they wouldn't vanish.

I reached the gate, my hair dripping, my clothes soaking. The rain wasn't cold, it was a welcome relief, but the creature that was being held in a now-sodden blanket could be imperilled by being out in this weather.

'Come inside,' I exclaimed, lifting the gate off its latch and flinging it wide open, my thoughts centred on getting the animal to safety. The person, who I now realised was a man, shook his head. He just stayed standing there.

I stopped.

'Come on, you're soaking and whatever you're holding must be wet through as well.'

Again, the man just stood there.

'I won't come in. Just take it.' His voice was rough-sounding, his manner shifty. I hesitated for a moment, wondering if I should be scared of him. Perhaps he meant us harm? Perhaps I should've brought Dan with me after all? But I never gave a thought for my own safety when an animal was in trouble. Perhaps it was time I did.

'You need to come inside and get whatever animal it is you're holding into warmth and safety,' I said, this time with authority. I could feel my anger rising now, as the rain hammered down, soaking us all further.

I wiped my wet hair off my face, strands of which were causing drips to run into my eyes. The man, a rather awkward-looking figure wearing an oversized Metallica T-shirt and faded scruffy jeans, both wet through, was standing rooted to the spot, as though he had something to say.

Suppressing my instinct to get the animal indoors and to get us all out of this downpour, I waited. Eventually my patience was rewarded.

'I can't keep her. I just can't do it. Having a dog wasn't what I expected.' The man's voice trailed off as lightning lit up the sky again.

'I tried, I really did . . .' His words trailed off.

Looking at this bedraggled man, I couldn't help but feel a prickle of distrust. Call it instinct, or just a feeling, but I wanted to get the dog and myself away from him as quickly as possible. I'd seen men like him before, men ready to cry crocodile tears for the kittens, puppies or even women they'd hurt or neglected, all too ready to atone for their sins. I knew I was sometimes too quick to pass judgement though; the man looked devastated, and as I didn't yet know what he had in his arms, I tried not to show him my disquiet.

Just then, the creature began to wiggle and I saw the distinctive face of a boxer puppy, its upturned nose, drooping jaw and the small ears that framed its little face, poke out of the wet blanket.

'Look, all that doesn't matter now. The dog will be well cared for with us. Let's just get the puppy inside!'

The man shook his head. His face was dark against the gloom of the sky, and his expression was a scowl.

'I'm not comin' in. Just take her and I can go.'

'Give her to me then, quickly,' I ordered. I knew I was dangerously close to losing my temper with him for keeping this bedraggled creature bundled up in the wet cloth for longer than was necessary, so that he could assuage his conscience.

'Just give her to me. I don't care what you've done to her, how she is. Just hand her over and you can go,' I said quietly. At that moment, a clap of thunder sounded overhead, making me jump, but my arms were held out and remained as steady as I could manage.

At long last, the man took a step towards me, and, more gently than I expected, he carefully placed the puppy into my arms. I smelled alcohol and cannabis on him, and, for a brief moment, I felt real pity for the man. I could see he didn't want to let the dog go, but it was also clear that he had trouble looking after himself, let alone an innocent puppy.

The little creature squirmed in my arms, and its movement broke the spell.

'Is she hurt? Sick?' My eyes bore into this man's. He stared back at me silently. He had short hair, an earring in one ear and his knuckles were tattooed. I didn't like the look of him, and something about him was starting to make me uneasy, even though he hadn't so much as set foot inside the gate area.

He turned without answering me.

'Close the gate behind you,' I said gruffly, backing off, just as Dan ran over.

'All okay here?' he asked, having noticed at once the set of my face.

'I'll tell you once we're indoors,' was all I said as we began the short dash back to my bungalow.

The man stayed standing there, his back to us, and for a horrible moment, I thought he might turn around and march up to reclaim the pup.

Only my fumbling attempts to open the door betrayed how shaken up I felt by this dog's dramatic entrance, and Dan, ever observant, noticed it at once.

'It isn't like you to feel unsettled.'

'No, it isn't, but there was something about him I didn't trust . . .' I said, glancing over at the CCTV cameras showing me views across the site. Dan and I stood there watching as the man, grainy on the camera film, eventually turned around, shut the gate behind him, got into his van and drove away.

FOUR

Terrified

Gently unwrapping the wet blanket revealed a quivering, shaking little boxer puppy with a black nose, and big shining dark eyes. My heart broke at the sight of her doleful-looking face staring up at me.

Her fur was very short and sleek, pale nut brown in colour, a white stripe running down her face. Despite her obvious distress, her long thin tail wagged furiously as she made little whining noises.

'Don't be scared, little one. You're safe here with us. Do you know where you are?' I peered down at her, the tiny creature licking my hand as I held her.

'You've arrived at the Barby Keel Animal Sanctuary, which is a very good place to be. We've got lots of people here who will take care of you, you know.'

The puppy appeared to be listening intently. Her head was bent slightly to one side, and her ears were pricked up as if trying to understand every word.

Just then Harry tried to poke his nose in and the puppy visibly recoiled.

'Out, Harry. Go on your bed. That's it. On your bed.' Harry gave me a look of disgust, then turned reluctantly and sloped off, his tail between his legs, clearly very aggrieved to be excluded. He was used to being my number one dog, and this newcomer seemed to have upset him more than the many others that had arrived at our door. Perhaps he sensed that this one might turn out to be special.

'You're a beautiful girl,' Dan remarked, reaching down to stroke her chest, which was a flash of white fur amid the deep brown of the rest of her body.

As soon as Dan moved towards her, the pup frantically scrambled away, burying herself close to me, her tiny body trembling.

'Oh dear, it's alright pup, Dan won't harm you. His bark is far worse than his bite,' I said softly, raising an eyebrow at my farm manager.

'She might just be frightened by me being a man,' Dan said. 'I've seen it before. If a pup is mistreated or hurt by an owner, at first they often find it difficult to cope when they're around someone of the same gender. It'll be a case of her learning to trust caring males again. Poor girl. She's thinner than I'd like to see, as well.'

I cuddled the small creature close. As I stroked her soft brown fur, wet from the downpour, I could feel the bones her ribs. She shivered with cold even though it was a warm day in spite of the storm, which had started to abate. The rain was less torrential now, and the thunder had passed overhead, though we could still hear the occasional rumble in the distance.

'What a dramatic entrance you made, beautiful girl. Now, let's get you dried off and then . . .' I gasped, unable to contain my shock at the sight.

I'd seen many things, dogs with bruises and suppurating wounds, cats with tumours eating away their faces, rabbits with claws so long they could cut themselves, but nothing so far had prepared me for the sight that greeted me.

The puppy's front leg was gone, and all that remained was a bloody, painful-looking stump that had clearly been left untreated.

'She's only got three legs!' I exclaimed. Dan, who had turned to walk away, stopped dead in his tracks.

We both looked down at the pup in my arms. I held her up so my farm manager could see more clearly. The dog shivered as I held her, but still tried to lick the end of my nose.

'It looks like it's infected,' Dan frowned, bending to look. 'Poor animal, it must be hurting her. How on earth did an injury like that happen to such a young dog?'

We looked at each other, the distress and shock mirrored between us. It was unusual to see a dog with a missing front leg. Until now, I'd only ever seen dogs with a back limb missing.

'How could someone just leave her like this?' I muttered, feeling a rush of anger towards the owner who had neglected this helpless, innocent creature. 'We'd better call the vet straight away. She looks like she'll need antibiotics and a dressing. You poor little thing. How did this happen to you, eh?'

As I spoke, I lay the pup gently down onto my lap. So, this was the reason she hadn't tried to leap out of my arms, or her previous owner's, for that matter. I'd assumed the dog was simply cowed by the experience of being dumped somewhere unfamiliar, but even if that played a part, I felt sure we'd discovered the real reason for this young puppy's meekness.

With a grimace, I looked again at the wound, which was covered in pus, and shook my head. Even if the owner had been ill-equipped to deal with a disabled dog, he should never have left it so long to get help.

I sighed, and the little dog seemed to wag her tail even harder. I couldn't help myself; I inwardly condemned the fact that her owner hadn't sought help for the injury earlier. It was always hard not to judge people, but this time I failed. I felt a surge of anger. Who could leave a puppy in this state? I had no idea if the owner had anything to do with the injury itself, but surely he could've brought this puppy to me before the wound became so infected.

I understood that taking on a puppy was like having a small child. They needed proper care, a steadfast routine and lots of attention. Some people just weren't able to give their dogs this, and in those cases, I was glad when they recognised it and had the sense to drop their animals with me. I had seen on the man's face how agonising the choice was, and I sensed that he'd realised how deeply he'd failed this scrap of a dog. My anger eased a little.

I stroked the pup's wet head as I waited for Dan to return with a towel to dry her off. Although it was something I'd seen all too often, I never got used to the sight of a neglected or hurt animal.

Many animals were dumped, abandoned or abused so badly they suffered starvation, disease or injury. Some were left because the owners got bored of them, some because the commitment of having a pet to care for was too much, and some because, like that sad-looking man, were simply incapable of taking on the responsibility of one of God's precious creatures.

This little dog summed up all the reasons I kept going, kept running the sanctuary although the days were long, the money tight and the stresses and strains a reality of each and every day. This little puppy, whose black eyes melted my heart from the moment I saw them, was the reason I did it, along with all the other abandoned creatures, and in that moment, as I sat quietly with her, I didn't regret a thing.

'Here you go – one dry towel.' Dan threw the towel at me from the doorway of my lounge.

'Hmm, have you lost the use of your legs too?' I teased, laughing at his apparent inability to walk across my small living room to deliver the towel.

'I've got things to do, Barby. The pup is in safe hands with you. If you need me, try me on the walkie-talkie and I'll do my best to ignore you.' Dan whistled as he walked off, leaving me chuckling. I enjoyed our banter, though it wasn't for everyone.

Then I remembered about the vet.

'Did you call Stephen?' I shouted after him, but he'd gone.

I tutted to the pup, who continued to gaze up at me. She was still trembling but less violently, and several times she'd licked my hand as I tickled her chin and stroked her perky little ears.

Being dumped was sadly an all-too-frequent occurrence, but there were times when people arrived with their animal and were able to give us a history of their dog or cat, and the reasons why they needed to be rehomed. We'd heard every excuse under the sun, though many owners, through poverty, tragedy and circumstances beyond their control, were forced to give up a beloved pet, causing great emotional distress.

More and more, we were encountering people who were forced to choose between their pet and their rented accommodation, as landlords were becoming increasingly strict about not allowing animals. Others had simply run out of money, or their pet required expensive treatment that they were unable to afford. Some just decided that having a pet wasn't for them. Obviously I had less patience for these people, but we all tried hard not to show our feelings to those who turned up at our door. My motley crew knew that it was vital that we take in every animal offered to us, even if they could never be rehomed due to behavioural issues, trauma or sickness. There would always be a home for an unwanted animal at the shelter, and though it meant we rarely had much money, and were always stretched beyond our means, it was the founding philosophy of the sanctuary.

I dried the puppy carefully, making sure not to go near the infected area.

'I reckon you're only just over a month old, far too young to have been taken from your mother. What were they thinking?'

By way of an answer, the dog moaned slightly, and leaned her head over, trying to lick the wound that was surely causing her pain.

'You're safe now, little one,' and even as I whispered reassuring words to the pup, shivering with cold, her tail between her legs, her ears back and her eyes now looking as forlorn and lost as I'd ever seen, I couldn't contain the anger I felt rising within me again. A sudden clap of thunder startled me out of my reverie.

'Don't worry, you're in better hands now,' I said firmly, trying to control my feelings and bring myself back to what mattered: this tiny pup and her poorly leg, or what was left of it. It did me no good to dwell on other people and their treatment of the animals left in my care, but I wasn't a saint. I was all too human, and I always struggled to keep my feelings under control when it came to the youngest, most vulnerable creatures.

If the puppy had been left with me 'properly', the owner would've filled out an extensive series of forms, describing every aspect of the dog's breed, character, behaviour and their circumstances: where they'd lived, how much room the puppy had had to play in, whether they were safe around children and other dogs, whether they'd been a rescue dog before ending up being rehomed again.

All of this information was vital to our centre. It helped us to understand what we might be dealing with, and how to give the animal the very best care and support. If the dog had shown behavioural problems, such as biting people, or barking excessively, or ripping up furniture, we could start the detective work, looking at how to heal the trauma or loss they may have suffered, or how their lack of basic training might be causing problems. We needed to know if they'd had a history of mistreatment or violence so that we could best protect the animal, and ourselves. We needed to know what food they ate, whether they had any allergies or any previous veterinary care. It was like building an entire profile, and any information an owner could provide helped us to piece together the complex jigsaw of an animal's previous life.

Without this vital information, we were going into it blind, as was the case of this pup in my arms. We had no idea what had happened to her in the past, or whethers she had existing illnesses or issues apart from the obvious injury to her leg.

As I pondered this, I felt softly down her body. Dan was right. There was too much of her ribcage visible, which could only mean that she hadn't been fed enough. If she hadn't received the correct nutrition as a baby, this might be disastrous, leading to a lifetime of compromised health. Further down her back, her fur felt matted, though it was very short, and she had some dandruff, which was a further sign that her nutrition had been poor. She was a sweet girl, desperate for affection even though she was scared.

'I bet you're hungry, you look half starved,' I said, once she was dry. I placed her gently down on the big leather sofa.

In the past, I would've kept my dog Teddy, a huge Irish wolfhound cross, away from this pup as well as Harry, shutting him outside while I took care of the new arrival, but my beloved companion had passed away in the spring, and although it was almost four months since he'd died of natural causes, I still looked for him when I awoke each morning, and mourned for him every night.

Teddy had been a rescue, like all the other dogs I'd ever owned. He was dumped in a large cardboard box by his owner, who was known only for the squeal of his tyres as he left so hastily, and the state of the loyal, playful, daft black-haired, straggly puppy that he left.

Terrified, trembling, bruised yet desperate for love, unwanted Teddy came into my life abruptly, and though I tried many times to rehome him, he kept bounding back.

He grew larger by the day, and would knock everything flying as he played. He refused to do his business outside the caravan I was living in at the time, and despite everything, despite all the breakages, disappointments and rehoming disasters, he was the ultimate doggie love of my life. We were destined to be together, and so, eventually, I gave in to the universe's plan for us both. He lived with me for many years, never leaving my side. My staff called him 'Barby's shadow' as he followed me everywhere. He was a scruffy, dark giant of a dog, with the biggest heart, whom everyone adored. The day he died was one of the darkest I've ever known. It was his heart that gave way. He was trotting towards me one fine summer day, at the grand old age of thirteen, when he stopped, looked me full in the eyes and collapsed. I think he was dead before he hit the grass under his paws.

That was mere months ago, and still the shock of Teddy's sudden passing haunted me. My nights had been spent feeling incredibly alone without his enormous body nestled up to me on my bed, though Harry had replaced him in that spot. I adored Harry, but somehow it wasn't the same. The days were full and demanded all my attention, so thankfully, I had barely a spare moment to grieve for him, but at night it was different. My sleep had all but vanished for the first month after his passing as I wept continually through the night till sunrise. My distress was so extreme that I thought about closing the sanctuary. I came within a hair's breadth of shutting the whole place down, so overwhelmed was I by his loss. Thankfully, the good people around me got me through and convinced me to keep going for Teddy's sake, but for weeks it was touch and go.

I was still reeling from the trauma of losing my beloved Teddy, and seeing this poor little pup in my arms, her large black eyes echoing those of Teddy's on the day he arrived, just as frightened, just as maltreated and dumped just as cruelly, brought the memories flooding back. As I sat there, holding the pup, I felt my heart open again to this new little dog, something that I had been scared of happening. Instinctively, I wanted to shut down my feelings immediately. I didn't ever want to feel pain like losing Teddy ever again, and I certainly didn't want a sweet, abandoned young puppy to reopen the emotional wounds that were still so fresh.

Just then the dog moaned and I realised I needed to call the vet straight away.

'I'll get you something to eat once the vet has been here, but he's the priority for you, little one.' As I spoke, she groaned softly again in pain.

I picked up my phone and dialled the number of Claremont Veterinary Practice in Sidley.

'Stephen? Yes, it's Barby, you must come now please – it's urgent.'

FIVE

Boxer Puppy

'You there?' Dad's gentle voice preceded the vet's. I looked up to see my father strolling into the lounge, the ease of his steps belying the fact that he was now in his nineties. That question was his signature entrance, so I always knew it was him coming in before I'd even set eyes on him.

He perched on the arm of the sofa as I sat in my favourite armchair with the puppy curled up on my lap. The dog raised her head to see who was there and gave a small wag of her long tail before settling down again. She didn't try to lick Dad's hand or ask for a stroke, and I saw then that Dan was right. This little girl had developed a fear of men, either as a result of whatever it was that had given her her stump, or through the lack of care given by her owner. Of course, I'd never know for sure.

My father was the sweetest, most compassionate and placid man I'd ever known, and I'd never seen an animal greet him with such little enthusiasm. Despite his gentle presence, the pup stared at him warily.

'She's a dear little thing, isn't she,' Dad said, his eyes twinkling behind his glasses. His grey hair had thinned over the years and his face was deeply lined, but he had an aura of calm and peace about him that usually made everyone – animal or human – warm to him immediately.

Dad didn't try to stroke the dog or pick her up, sensing that the pup needed more time to get used to him. It was so like my father to hold back and let the animal come to him.

'Did Dan tell you?' I asked, without elaborating.

Dad nodded his response. 'The poor girl has a front leg missing. The amputation looks a bit of a bodge job, or so Dan says,' he said, smiling at the pup who managed another wag of her tail before sighing and creeping further into my lap.

'I think she's had a big shock, probably a car accident, judging by her manner and she's also very wary of males, though I can hardly blame her!'

I smiled a little as I spoke. I didn't mean it, of course, but I did like to joke with my workers, saying it took two men to do the work of one woman. That always went down well with Dan, who would snort in outrage, then offer to leave the back-breaking work to me.

'So, she's a boxer then. Lovely dogs, though they need lots of exercise and lots of love. This one won't have thrived if she was left alone a lot,' Dad said companionably.

He turned to the pup, slowly holding out his hand for the dog to sniff. The little soul sniffed it then gave it an exploratory lick.

'Progress already, see!' Dad beamed. 'My hunch is that this girl has been taken from its mum too soon and then left, cooped up indoors, lonely and probably afraid.'

I sighed. 'That's my instinct too. Boxers are usually so gregarious, especially as puppies; it would take a lot of unhappiness to make them look as sad as this one does.'

'Don't forget she's probably in pain with her leg too, or what's left of it. You may find that once Stephen has got to grips with the infection, she'll be much more like a normal puppy, getting into mischief, and bounding all over the place – if she can,' Dad observed, looking at me kindly. He knew the emotional toll each fostered animal took on me, particularly when mistreatment may have been involved, and as I'd lost Teddy quite recently, the grief of that was raw still.

I returned Dad's loving gaze as steadily as I could, but tears were threatening to fall. His blue eyes saw everything, as they always did. He had a kind of sixth sense when it came to understanding both animals and humans. He knew that seeing this pup would bring back memories for me, and bring me as much heartache as it did satisfaction in being able to help.

'I know it's not the first puppy we've had in since Teddy passed, but I think this is the first one that has really reminded you of him,' Dad said, looking down at his hands. His voice was barely above a whisper. 'It's bound to upset you but you need to focus on this dog. She's not Teddy.'

'I know that,' I bit back, and immediately regretted it. 'Sorry, Dad,' I added, looking over at him sheepishly.

He smiled at me, never taking offence. My father was a quiet man, a man born to tend the earth and care for animals. He wasn't interested in money or status. He had worked all his life in order to provide for us, and for the continuous stream of animals he had rescued over the years. He never wanted anything for himself; in fact, he still lived in a caravan on my site, which he'd made his home twenty years ago.

I'd lived in a caravan too when my first house was bulldozed for lack of planning permission. It took me many years to get over the shock of it, and many years of living in a draughty, leaking caravan, before I plucked up the courage to build my own place again, this time with full permission and built of solid bricks and mortar.

It was a humble home. Like my father, I cared nothing for wealth or material things. Animals were my passion, and my reason for being, just like him, and so I'd built a small bungalow with one upstairs room for myself. It had a small kitchen, and a lounge which contained a cabinet filled to the brim with evidence of my second passion: darts trophies and shields won over the years. The bungalow had a single bedroom, where I sleep with Harry and Ted, of course, until his passing, and a tiny office. That was it. It was all I needed. Dad was happier staying in his caravan and so we lived side by side in complete harmony. My father had left my mother many years ago, and as a result, I rarely, if ever, saw my mother. There was bad blood between us. She disliked me, and I resented her. She had preferred my brother Peter as a child, and shown me in every possible way that I was inferior to him. Though I secretly agreed with her, I never forgave her for not loving me the way a mother should. As soon as I could support myself, I left home, and Dad soon came with me. He'd never left, and so we'd rubbed along, adding to our menagerie in my small one-bedroom flat in the Sussex town where I was born, until I bought this land, and my real story, that of saving and fostering animals, began.

I looked over at my father, who was watching the dog as it lay close to me. Was it my imagination or had he aged recently? Where once he would have been out on the land digging ditches, hammering in stakes to make fences or lugging sacks of animal feed around the site, now he preferred to potter in his caravan, or pet the horses in his gentle way. His back had stooped, and his skin looked almost translucent, but whenever I enquired about his health, he always answered the same way: 'I'm fine, don't you worry about me.'

He caught my eye at that moment and saw me eyeing him.

'Barby, I'm fine . . .' he started to say, before I inter-rupted, finishing his sentence: 'Don't you worry about me!' I grinned.

'Cheeky. You always were so cheeky,' he laughed, but neither of us could deny the fact that he wasn't as fit or as able as he had been even just a year ago.

Before I could say anything further, there was a knock on the door, and a familiar voice said: 'Barby, it's me . . .'

'Stephen, thank you for coming. We've got a real sorry case here,' I said as the vet strode into my lounge. The room itself wasn't big, but there was enough room for two sofas for my volunteers to have their morning coffee on, my favourite armchair and an open fire for the cold evenings.

Stephen, a young man with dark hair, a short stature and a broad grin, threw his vet bag on one of the leather couches and turned his attention immediately to the dog on my lap.

Without so much as a 'hello', he quickly got to work. He didn't move the pup from my lap, but checked her all over, reaching for his stethoscope to listen to the puppy's heart, which I could feel racing in my hands.

'Let's have a look at what remains of her leg. Barby, please hold her still. She may not like this, but I need to get a proper look at the wound.'

Stephen was firm, but I never doubted him. He was an extremely able, utterly devoted vet whose passion for animals rivalled my own. We understood each other, and he would always go out of his way to come to our site to see a creature in need.

When he caught sight of the injured leg, his face crumbled.

'It's bad, isn't it?' I asked, holding my breath as I watched his expression.

Stephen shook his head and for a moment my heart soared at the thought that the pup wasn't as bad as he thought. That hope was dashed immediately.

Stephen was shaking his head in disgust.

'I've seen worse amputations, but this looks like it was done on the cheap. The dog must be in a lot of pain. There's definitely infection in there as I'm sure you've gathered, as it hasn't had time to heal. Whoever was looking after her clearly didn't care for her properly.

'I guess she's only a month old; far too young to have been through all this. I see situations like this all too often, and there's often irresponsible dog breeding at the root of it. I understand people need to try and make a living, but I wish they'd keep hold of the pups until they're old enough to leave their mothers. This one was probably rehomed before she was even a month old.'

Stephen shook his head in disgust before continuing: 'She'll need a course of antibiotics for sure. She's got a fever but that should be dealt with by the medication. Apart from that, she just needs a lot of loving kindness.'

I nodded in agreement: 'Well, she'll get plenty of that here. And look, here comes the motley crew ready for their break. I'm sure they'll be cooing over her in no time.'

As I spoke, the door opened again and a stream of volunteers, young and old, traipsed through. Some were kind enough to take off their wellies, some just walked straight in, leaving a muddy trail across the carpet. I wasn't house-proud at all, but even so, I preferred them to keep the soil outdoors.

The first to enter the lounge with a steaming hot cup of tea in her hand was my longest-serving volunteer and great friend, Diane. Di had blonde wispy hair, covered by the woolly hat she wore all year round. She was wearing a dark green fleece, a pair of old, grey cotton trousers and I couldn't help but notice that her wellies were resolutely still affixed to her feet.

'You didn't take your boots off then?' I asked, as sternly as I could.

'I didn't, Barby. Am I going to get a telling-off?' she replied, her eyebrows raised as she returned my gaze just as sternly.

We glared at each other for a moment longer before both breaking into chuckles.

'As if you care about a bit of mud.' She grinned, settling onto the sofa beside me.

'I don't, but if everyone kept their wellies on it'd be a quagmire in here.'

'Lucky it's just me then,' Di laughed. 'Do you want a cuppa, Barby? Stephen, can I get you anything?'

'Not for me, Diane,' replied Stephen. He had finished his examination of the puppy and was packing away his equipment.

'And who's this gorgeous little lady?' asked Di. 'What a lovely girl.'

'She's a sweetheart, but she's been through the mill,' I replied, holding the dog to me protectively.

Diane leaned over and gave the pup a gentle stroke. Her big doleful eyes gazed up at her and she whined a little.

'Barby, here's a prescription,' Stephen said, interrupting our conversation and flourishing a piece of paper in my direction. 'Will you or one of your volunteers be able to pick it up today? This puppy needs the pills straight away.'

'I can go,' Diane piped up immediately. 'Just let me finish this tea and I'll get a lift with you back into Sidley, assuming you're going that way?'

'I'll drop you at the surgery then carry on, as I have to go on into Bexhill.' The vet nodded. Turning to me, he continued, 'Barby, please call me tomorrow and let me know how she's doing, especially if there's no change in the fever.'

I nodded, knowing that Stephen would reappear tomorrow afternoon or evening as he liked to see for himself how the more vulnerable patients were getting on. I thanked my lucky stars every day to have such a wonderful vet helping us at the sanctuary. We spent a small fortune on the bills but we knew our animals were extremely well cared for, and that was all that mattered to me.

'You can tell me what's wrong with her on the way,' Di chipped in.

'Who's this little angel, then?' said a young girl, who looked to me to be barely out of her teen years. She had green dyed hair, a nose stud and a sleeve of colourful tattoos decorating her arm. She also happened to be one of our gentlest and most reliable volunteers, helping out every week in between her studies. I'd only met her a handful of times as she preferred to take her breaks in the cattery area, but today she had appeared with the rest of them and was staring intently at the tiny puppy curled up in my lap, staring up at her dolefully with her big, dark eyes.

'She doesn't have a name yet. She was abandoned here this morning before you lot arrived for work.' As I spoke, I glanced up at my dad, who had been silent throughout the vet's visit, listening closely. Somehow, it felt fitting that Dad should be the one to choose the pup's moniker.

'What do you think, Dad?' I asked quietly.

For a moment, Dad didn't speak, but then said, 'I think she has a rather regal look about her. Even though she's poorly, she still holds her head up high. How about calling her Princess?'

'Princess,' echoed Stephen, 'that's a fine name for a Boxer. Alright, I'll put Princess on her records, and I'll no doubt see you all tomorrow.' With that, the vet left, along with Diane.

I looked down at the tiny pup. Even though she was shivering and unwell, her head was cocked to the side as if she was listening to every word we were saying.

I stroked her soft brown ears gently.

'Hello, Princess, welcome to the Barby Keel Animal Sanctuary.'

SIX

Safety

I awoke the next morning to find the sun already up. It was past six, and the sanctuary was coming to life. Outside the bedroom window, there was a cacophony of sound coming from the pens, kennels, fields and runs across the site. I had a few cockerels who crowed from four o'clock, and once they started, they seemed to set off a domino effect of noise. The sheep baaaed, the donkeys brayed, the horses whinnied, the geese and chickens clucked and clattered across the yard, their clawed feet tapping on the concrete, and the dogs barked their response, demanding their breakfast.

To me, it was normal, but as I yawned and stretched, I glanced over at my latest charge, who I had put to sleep in the bathroom area behind a baby gate to keep her separate from Harry, and could see the puppy was quaking behind her temporary prison bars.

Although it had been weeks now, I still couldn't help but look for Teddy each morning when I awoke. Somehow, in that space between dreaming and waking, I always felt certain I could feel his large, heavy presence next to me on the bed; his deep breathing; his yawns and sighs as he awoke, then his joy at being next to me and the new day starting. Every day I woke and looked to my right to see him and every day I realised afresh that he wasn't there, and my heart sank once again. Grief was a strange thing. It kept catching me unawares. One minute I'd think I was fine, accepting that Teddy was in a better place, and comforted by the knowledge that I'd see him again one day on Rainbow Bridge, the place where humans and animals are reunited. But on other days, it was like being floored by a tidal wave of pain and loss, and each morning I felt the grief wash over me as I remembered that Teddy was gone.

Yet this morning had been different.

I had looked for Teddy, but was immediately diverted by the pup that needed my care and attention. It was the first time I hadn't had that rush of sadness upon waking since Ted had died.

Before I'd had a chance to process the shift in my grieving, I'd pulled on a T-shirt and jeans and stepped over the baby gate and into the small bathroom area that Princess had spent the night in.

The two of us been up half the night as the antibiotics Stephen had prescribed needed to be administered every two hours. Princess really should've gone into our specially constructed kennels overnight, but her face had been so pitiful, her expression so confused and sad, that I had gone against our protocol and taken her in with me.

The fact that she was running a temperature and needed the antibiotics so regularly was another reason to keep her in with me. The thought of having to spend the night sitting in one of the uncomfortable plastic chairs in the cold kennel building, dozing for two hours then giving her her medicine, had not been a pleasant thought and so I'd refused all offers of help from my staff and kept her in my home.

After a little stroke and a few reassuring words, it was time for her medicine. By now, Princess was used to the routine, but that didn't stop her from struggling at the sight of the oral syringe filled with antibiotics. I tried to hold her mouth still but she yawned, a sign of distress in dogs, and obstinately pulled her face away.

'Please don't turn away, you daft animal. I'm trying to help you,' I said in a tone of gentle exasperation. There was no way of explaining to her that she wasn't receiving another cruelty, but that she had in fact, found a safe haven. It would take time for her to learn that she was safe and that she could trust us, and in the meantime, I had to be patient.

Princess was having none of it, though. I put the syringe down and held her in my arms instead but she knew what was coming and tried to wriggle free. She made little whining noises and yawned again.

'I know this is stressful for you but if the vet says you have to have it then that's that. You don't want the infection to spread, do you? You have to be a brave girl and let me do this.' At long last, I managed to clasp her mouth open and squirt the liquid inside, shutting her jaws and trying to hold her still until she swallowed. Finally, she gave a great gulp and I could let her go.

Princess didn't attempt to move away from me, instead she slumped back down onto the bed of soft blankets I'd made for her, staring up at me grumpily.

I had to laugh at the sight of her. Her face showed her disgust with me, but nevertheless, her tail wagged enthusiastically as I stroked the lovely rich brown of her sleek fur. Apart from the infected wound and her lack of body weight, she didn't seem to be in a terrible condition. She had obviously been looked after to a certain extent, though perhaps not as well as I would've liked, and at least she had received some veterinary care, even if it hadn't been of the highest quality.

I'd noticed yesterday that she didn't attempt to explore her surroundings or have a sniff around, as I would have expected from a puppy so young. She was obviously in pain from her amputated leg, and it looked as though she hadn't yet tried walking on the three legs she did have.

'Princess, you're going to have to get used to having your medicine if you want to grow up to be a big strong boxer dog.' I smiled, making her ears prick up in response. She was a very affectionate girl, that much was already evident. She loved being stroked and tickled under her chin and down the white stripe of fur that covered her chest.

In situations where a dog has been neglected or abused, or with animals like Princess where we couldn't be sure what had happened to them in the past, we used various methods to create a feeling of safety, and to try to prevent them from feeling overwhelmed.

I hadn't let anyone else apart from me and the vet touch Princess. I knew I was becoming a little too emotionally involved with this animal. By rights, she should've been taken to the kennels when she arrived but I'd insisted she sleep with me in my bungalow; I was overseeing every aspect of her care, which would normally have been left to one of the dog volunteers. I knew I was falling for this little scrap, but I couldn't stop myself. Some animals just made a profound impression on me, and Princess was one of them.

It was always best to hold back and let a dog come to you, as Dad had, rather than to force cuddles or attention onto them. Dogs could be triggered to withdraw or become aggressive by misplaced attention, and both for our own safety, and that of the animal, we had to take a careful, slow approach to caring for them. It was a case of building trust and letting the dog understand that we posed no threat to them. It wasn't easy to hold back, especially when we were dealing with an animal in pain, but I knew that some animals weren't used to receiving love or attention – a fact that never failed to break my heart – and therefore they might need time to adjust to gentle, loving contact as opposed to the harsh words or beatings they'd grown used to.

I had no idea if Princess had suffered either of those things, but even if she hadn't, she'd been through a terrible accident, so bad that she'd had to have her leg amputated, and so I knew she would've experienced some level of trauma as a result of that. I'd taken Princess in my arms without a struggle when she'd first arrived, and the fact she'd curled up on my lap as well were both good signs that she was able to cope with human contact and affection.

My knees started to hurt as I crouched, so I raised myself up slowly so as not to alarm the pup. As I did so, I caught sight of myself in my bathroom mirror. I had always been a slim woman with bleached white-blonde hair, though over the years I'd put on a bit of weight. I didn't mind. I valued my body for the work it could do, lifting crates and sacks of feed, rather than what it looked like. A few extra pounds gave me strength.

Time spent working outside on the land in the sun and wind had given me a permanently semi-tanned glow, though my face was lined. My hair, which had turned a dark shade of blonde now that I'd stopped bleaching it lighter, was peppered with strands of grey, which I looked at wistfully. I was a woman in my early sixties so some grey hair was to be expected, but I hated the thought of getting older, not because of vanity – I didn't care about my looks – but because the older I got, the less I would be able to look after the animals in our care.

I have never been a vain woman, caring nothing for fancy clothes or the creams and potions women pay good money for. I have always thought that any money not spent on rescuing animals was a waste, and so I still used the old-fashioned Pond's cream on my face when I remembered, and no make-up whatsoever.

My T-shirt had seen better days, and my jeans were ripped. I laughed as I saw myself, the big dark bags under my eyes revealing the lack of sleep I'd had.

'Well, none of the animals I look after give a damn what I look like, so it really doesn't matter!' I chuckled to myself.

At that moment, Diane popped her head round the door. I'd heard the kettle being flicked on from the kitchen a few feet away. Di had been a volunteer at the sanctuary for more years than I cared to remember. She'd turned up one day with her parents, bringing some cat food to donate to the sanctuary. I'd met her at the gate, and invited them all in for a cup of tea – and Diane never really left. From that day, she was a frequent and regular volunteer, coming up every weekend to help with the cattery, which she now ran. When her parents died, it was the sanctuary she turned to, leaving her job and coming to work here on a full-time basis. She was one of the most caring, loyal people I'd ever met, and she could remember every animal, every creature that had ever stayed at the shelter.

'You're finally up then? It's almost half past six, Barby.' Di grinned, her hair a tangle around her beaming face. 'Harry's already gone out without you. I saw him walking round by the kennels.'

'You mind your cheek. I needed a lie-in because I've been up all night with this little scrap of dog,' I said stoutly, 'and yes, Harry has got the grumps again. Best to leave him to it. I think he feels usurped, and I'd love a cuppa. You know how I like it . . .'

'I do, Barby: strong with four sugars. Very bad for you, you know.'

A couple of minutes later, I was still sitting and chatting quietly to Princess when Di appeared with my cup of tea and her morning coffee.

'Do you want me to make your breakfast or will you be able to leave Princess for long enough?' Di arched her eyebrow at me. She knew my propensity to fall in love with the dogs that found their way here.

I chuckled. 'I'll tear myself away, thank you. Are you busy today, dear?' I asked companionably.

Diane was always busy, as we all were. There was a seemingly endless list of jobs that needed doing each day: feeding the five hundred or so animals, brushing them, cleaning them out, sweeping the yard, carrying feed around, making fences, repairing equipment and buildings, answering the seemingly endless phone calls that came in each day, organising cat and dog rehoming, sorting home checks for potential foster families and last, but by no means least, fundraising to keep the sanctuary going, something that was a full-time job in itself.

'Well, we have one hundred and twenty cats in at the moment, so I've got a couple of volunteers to help with cleaning them out and feeding them while I check on the poorly cats and give them their medicine. We really must look at building a new cattery hospital or extending the one we have, Barby. We're desperate for more space.'

Di sipped her coffee and shrugged. She knew as well as I did that funds were tight at the moment, but this was nothing new; in fact, they were always tight.

'I know, dear, but at the moment there just isn't the money for a project as big as that. We did well at the Summer Fair so we're okay until Christmas for the day-to-day running, but anything beyond that is a bit of a stretch. Still, best not to worry, something always comes up,' I said. 'We always find the cash somehow, and it's not as if we're going to shut and kick all the animals out. We have to be optimistic, for their sakes at least.'

At that, we both looked down at Princess, who looked back at us with those huge doleful eyes.

'All that matters today is getting this girl back on her three paws. Though I am a bit worried that that's not going to happen,' I sighed.

'Why's that, Barby?' Di asked, knowing I often needed to chew over my thoughts aloud.

'Well, she hasn't tried to move herself from the bed since I put her there last night. Understandably, she hates the medicine, so she wriggles and makes a fuss about that, but she hasn't tried to explore the bathroom, make any mischief or sniff in the corners. I think she's scared of moving on just three legs. The injury is obviously recent, and I wonder if she's just not used to walking without the fourth?'

Di knew how much I took the animals and their suffering to heart. Princess's plight had touched me deeply, and already I was more emotionally involved with her and her progress than I would've liked to admit to.

'You won't know until the antibiotics kick in and her stump starts to heal, Barby. Until then, you'll just have to be patient, although I know it was never one of your virtues.' Di grinned.

I shot her a filthy look back before dissolving into giggles.

Di was right, of course. If you want a battleaxe to fend off a threat, then I'm your woman, but if you want a patient, calm person, then perhaps not.

'Seriously, though. We won't know how badly shocked or traumatised Princess has been until the medicine starts to do its job. Try not to get upset before you know what you're dealing with.

'She seems like a lovely puppy. She's probably a bit in shock and feeling pain right now, and it's why she's huddled down. She also might not have been given much affection before and that will no doubt be confusing to her.'

Those words were like a stab in my heart, but I knew Di was right. Only time would tell how badly Princess had been hurt, and whether or not she would ever be able to walk again without pain. Whatever happened, I knew I would stay with her, day and night, to give her all the love and care she needed. I knew it was partly my grief at losing Teddy that was making me connect so closely to this little creature, but I also knew that the sight of an animal in pain was something I never wished to see. Whatever I needed to do to get this girl well, I would do without a second thought. If I needed to stay up all night every night for a week, I would do it. I held the little puppy close to my chest, feeling her small heart beating against mine.

'I'm sorry for everything that has happened to you, Princess, but know this: you have found safety, and we will love you back to health and happiness. That is my promise to you,' I whispered. Di walked away, smiling back at me as she went.

Princess looked up at me as I deposited her back onto the blankets, and put out a paw which I stroked, and as if by magic, she rolled onto her side revealing her white belly, waiting for me to stroke her.

'You see,' I exclaimed, 'a miracle already!'

SEVEN

Getting Better

'Come on, Princess, that's it, try to get up. There's a good girl! See, now you're standing and you didn't think you'd manage that, did you! It's just a case of trusting that your remaining legs will carry you forwards. I know it feels strange, just keep going, little one . . .'

I beamed down at the puppy standing in front of me, shaking a little with the effort of standing upright. It broke my heart knowing that a dog of her age would normally be bounding around, getting into all sorts of mischief, with a real zest for life. Boxers are a breed that generally need lots of walking and exercise to curb their natural enthusiasm and energy, and so being disabled in the way Princess was would go profoundly against their nature.

I couldn't imagine how it felt to be inside Princess's body and mind, wanting desperately to play, to run free, and yet not knowing how.

'It's either the shock of the accident where she lost her

leg, or she's really struggling to understand how to move with a leg missing,' Dan sighed, a pained look on her face.

'Or a mixture of both,' I added.

Dan and I were standing in my lounge, trying to coax Princess into play. She'd been with us for a week, and each day she'd visibly improved as the antibiotics did their work. On the third day, after she'd greeted me with licks and cuddles when I climbed over the gate to bring her a dose, I'd decided to free her, hoping that she might limp off, ready to explore. I knew that Harry had decided to ignore the pup so there would be no problem there.

My hopes were dashed almost instantly.

Princess had done nothing. She'd lain there in her cosy blankets, clearly happy to see me, her tail wagging, her snuffles and licks proof that she was settling in nicely and starting to feel less pain, but she hadn't made any effort to move, apart from to use the litter tray beside her.

'I won't force you out. You can explore in your own time,' I'd said to her, stroking her lovely brown head and letting her chew at my hand softly, but we have to get you moving now that you're starting to heal.'

I smiled at her funny little square-shaped head, the way her short, folded-over ears pricked up and her beautiful eyes peered out of her dark face inquisitively.

'You're an intelligent girl, I can see that,' I mused. I could see her looking round, head cocked, taking in everything around her. Her breed was known as being clever and playful, even though they were originally bred as working dogs, developed in Germany in the nineteenth century as bull-baiting dogs. They would also be used to control cattle in slaughterhouses, and were one of the first breeds to be worked as police dogs. It's said their name comes from the sparring games boxers play when with other dogs. Whether it's true or not, they always need lots of companionship both with other dogs and humans. If this one had been kept alone, as we suspected from her unhappy condition, then she would've suffered greatly.

I didn't like to think of that. It was important to move forward at times like this, and not dwell on the past, however tempting.

'There's so much we'll never know about you,' I'd told her sadly. 'And so much that you can't tell us. We'll just have to muddle through somehow.'

Dogs are descended from wolves. They are pack animals, and most don't do well on their own, though some deal with it better than others. We were Princess's pack now, and it was my responsibility to encourage her out of her isolation and back into 'normal' dog behaviour, playing and mock-fighting, and exploring our boundaries in relative freedom.

When a dog doesn't leap at the chance to run free, I know, with a sinking heart, that they have been left in isolation long enough to retrain their doggie brain into giving up their instincts. It takes a lot of time alone to make a boxer puppy want to withdraw, though this one, of course, had the additional trauma of the injury.

Over the next few days, I'd enticed her out with treats and bones, hoping her permanent hunger would overcome her trepidation. By now, we were feeding her the appropriate amount of food for a puppy of her size, but I could only imagine that food had been scarce with her previous owner, because she always descended upon any meal or treat as though she was ravenous. To my relief, I had had some small successes.

The first time she tried to move, she got up as if expecting to have the use of her fourth leg and promptly fell down flat onto her face, clearly not used to this strange new lack of balance.

'Poor Princess, poor girl,' I cajoled, 'but we must never give up. Even if you fall down a hundred times, I'll be here to help you back up again.'

Princess whined, struggled back into a sitting position and bobbed her head down to sniff round at the site of her stump. The wound was healing nicely, but the vet had told us to stop her from licking it in case it got infected again during treatment. I'd decided not to put a cone on her as the wound had responded so quickly to the antibiotics, but that meant that I did need to keep a vigilant eye on her. I quickly put my hand out to stop her.

'Look this way, girl, come on, let's try that again.'

I walked back to the kitchen to grab a sausage from last night's dinner. If this didn't tempt her, nothing would.

I crouched a few steps away from her, dangling the tasty morsel in front of me. Princess's attention was suddenly focused entirely on the meat. A large dollop of drool slid out of her mouth, suspended jelly-like, hovering a couple of inches from the ground.

'That's it, good girl, now come and get it.'

I waved the sausage at her.

Finally, the temptation became too much. Princess moved, though she shuffled his way forward on her bottom until she reached me and the snack. She wolfed it down in two gulps.

'Well that's progress of a sort,' I said, smiling at the dear little thing. She may only have been a month or two old but already she had the regal look that boxers tend to have.

She sat and looked at me now, her head high and her back rigid though her white paws looked huge compared to her small body. She was such a comical-looking pup, I had to laugh. As I chuckled, she stretched her head over, her eyes big in her little face and her mouth turning down under the folds of skin at either side.

'What a sweetie you are. How could anyone neglect you, eh girl?' I curled up on the rug next to her, stroking her ears gently, feeling the fur smooth under my palms.

I sat with her for a while, giving her some of Teddy's old toys to chew on. She growled and shook a fluffy grey elephant that had seen better days.

'That's it, kill!' I giggled, relieved to see that she still had some of the instincts of a normal puppy. 'Kill that terrifying cuddly toy.'

The next day, I repeated the exercise of luring Princess up with the promise of food. This time I had a plate of ham in my hands. Princess looked up, sniffing the air as I approached.

'Can you smell the meat? This will be so tasty, Princess. Come and get it, come on . . .' I coaxed.

She looked at me, turning her head as she was curled up on the blankets, the only evidence of her having moved in the past few hours being the litter tray with fresh pee in it.

'I'll change the litter once you've tried some of this lovely ham. I bet it smells good, doesn't it, girl?'

Princess's face betrayed her desire. Where I would have expected a normal, healthy puppy to have run up, tail flying, paws gawky and clumsy as it bounded, this little pup looked like she was thinking about it, weighing up whether the effort to get to the feast would be worth it.

'You know you want it,' I murmured, moving a fraction of an inch closer to her.

Her nose was twitching. A great globule of drool was forming at her mouth, yet still she didn't move. Then suddenly, she lurched forward, dragging her bottom along the floor, working his back legs underneath her.

'That doesn't look at all comfortable, silly mutt,' I grumbled fondly. This certainly hadn't been what I'd envisaged when I thought about encouraging Princess to find a way to walk despite her injury.

'It's certainly efficient,' I giggled as she ate the ham with relish, dribble flying everywhere, 'but you're going to have to find a way to limp and to learn how to walk without that front leg, do you understand me?' I whispered to her gently.

It was the first time I'd seen a dog with a front leg amputated; it was much more usual to have a back leg removed after trauma, a road accident or because of a tumour.

The recovery of a dog with this type of major surgery would always be more difficult for the animal, more disabling, because of the trouble they would have with finding their centre of balance again. Standing or sitting would be problematic, even lying in the 'down' position would be tricky because dogs use their elbows to hold their heads up. I knew that Princess's journey would be harder, and that made my sympathy for her all the greater.

When she'd finished the ham, she planted her head back down on her paw, and shuffled back to the blankets in the seclusion that was so unusual for her breed.

After that, I moved her blankets into the lounge so that she could shuffle around in a more sociable space.

The urge to hide is a sign of trauma in a dog. Anxiety and shaking, panting and isolating were all classic signs, and ones that Princess had exhibited in the days she'd spent with us. However, each day she seemed a little brighter and more affectionate, but I knew that whatever she'd suffered would take years to heal completely.

Princess couldn't tell me what had happened to her before her arrival here. She couldn't tell me what her owner was like, how old she'd been when separated from her mother, or what had happened to her to result in such a terrible amputation. Some dogs become aggressive after trauma whereas some, like Princess, simply hide away, terrified of any contact with humans or animals.

Princess was still more reticent with males, though the calm presence of my father had made a definite improvement in that area. Just after I'd brought Princess out of the bathroom and into my living room, placing her on the floor close to me, Dad wandered in and sat near to her, though he was careful not to get too close. He sat there quietly humming to himself as he folded up a stack of raffle tickets for our Christmas Bazaar, which although months away, required a huge amount of preparation. Princess eyed him from her bed, yawning now and then to show she was feeling stressed.

'It's okay, girl, it's just Dad. She won't harm you,' I told her gently as I leafed through my big black book that contained all the numbers of people looking to adopt various animals. A pair of Siamese cats needed to be rehomed, and as they were siblings, we needed to place them together. As a rule, we tried to never separate cats that had been brought in together. I was passionate about that. Often people would try and sway me, saying it was better to rehome one of a pair rather than keep them both at the sanctuary, but I was adamant. To my way of thinking, it was cruel to separate them. The only exception had been one time when a litter of eight kittens came to us. It would've been impossible to rehome them all at once so they went to new owners in pairs.

'Hmm, I wonder if that lady who came in last Sunday would like a pair of cats. She said she liked Siamese cats,' I muttered to myself as I worked. I glanced up and noticed that Dad was crouching down next to Princess's bed. I stared at him in surprise, my glasses dangling off the end of my nose. What on earth was Dad doing? Didn't he realise he might upset the pup?

I held my breath for a moment, about to reproach Dad, but I was startled when Princess suddenly shuffled forward. She moved again slowly until she was almost next to my father.

'Lovely girl, who's a sweet puppy, eh?' crooned Dad. I watched as the dog leaned her head forward and let Dad give her a stroke. It seemed like a small move, but I knew it was a huge leap forward psychologically.

'Oh well done, Princess,' I said, my heart bursting with pride. 'What a brave puppy you are.' I couldn't resist her sweet little face and I bent down and scooped her up, taking care not to touch her stump. Very carefully, I lay her on my lap and as I did so, she licked my face and her tail went like the clappers.

Dad smiled over at me, his eyes twinkling.

'Progress,' was all he said.

Days passed. Princess had been with us for almost two weeks, and it was clear the medicine was doing its job. Every day, Princess was more alert, more affectionate, and had even shuffled over to Dad several more times for a stroke and a tickle under her chin. To my relief, the infection had gone from her amputation and the wound was healing up. It still looked red and raw, but it was much improved.

Once I was reassured that Princess was getting better, my thoughts turned to my father. He was ninety-five years old, yet he still had all his faculties. He was mobile, able to live independently and, as far as I knew, in relatively good health. Still, I couldn't help but think that another winter in his caravan couldn't be a good thing.

'You should be living inside the house,' I said one day as we sat together, me looking through the year's accounts, Dad taking a break from helping with the cats. Even though the long summer days seemed like they would go on forever, I'd already caught the first nips of autumn chill first thing in the morning as I went to feed our resident seagulls.

Each morning at six o'clock, a flock of gulls, crows, jays and small garden birds would gather, alighting onto the electricity wires that looped over the sanctuary, looking like a scene from the Hitchcock film *The Birds*. More and more would come each day, until the sky was filled with white, grey and black wings, and the air rang out with the screams and screeches of birds in motion. On squally days when the wind was fresh and the clouds raced across the sky, their feathers ruffled as they swayed on those pylon lines; on settled days they would sit there quietly, scanning the landscape and patiently waiting for their breakfast.

Every day, Diane or I would go out at the appointed time to feed them, carrying a large crate filled with stale bread. It took what felt like hours each day to break up the crusts and get it ready so that the birds could swoop down and take what they needed.

In all the years we'd performing this morning ritual, there had never been a point where the birds had attacked us for the bread or tried to alight on the crate as we carried it, a fact I found quite strange.

That morning, I'd carried out the food, placed it down on the field close to the entrance to the horses' paddock and watched as they descended in a flurry of wings and beaks. I shivered. The mornings had been hot and humid, hence the recent storms, but now there was a new clarity to the haze, a sharpness in the breeze that was the first sign of the season changing.

'You need to be inside, Dad. It's not good for you to keep living in your caravan – you're getting too old!'

I looked over at my beloved father. He had wisps of white hair framing his face. His eyes still twinkled bright blue, but he looked thinner and was starting to stoop. As always, he was well dressed in a striped shirt with the sleeves rolled up, ready for work, and a pair of sturdy boots and trousers.

He smiled as he returned my gaze. 'Don't worry yourself, Barby, I'm fine,' he insisted as always, before returning to his work.

Princess was sitting next to him on the sofa, a new habit she'd developed and one that we'd all remarked upon as being another huge step forward in her confidence. I would have to pick Princess up and deposit her there, but she sat happily, occupying herself as a steady stream of volunteers cooed over her. The puppy still hadn't made any effort to walk, despite the improvement to her leg, instead preferring to nuzzle into her bed, chew at her toys and pretend to play-fight from whatever position she was in with a particularly fierce fluffy dinosaur.

I was thrilled that Dad's quiet nature had won the pup over, but underneath his gentleness, he also had a mischievous side and was known throughout the sanctuary for his love of practical jokes. For a gentle man, he had rather a wicked sense of humour, which came out in funny ways.

That morning, for instance, I'd gone to the cutlery drawer to grab a knife to butter my toast and, to my surprise, found it full of socks. After taking a moment to register my confusion, I grinned. 'Daaaaad,' I said, looking round to see where on earth he'd hidden the knives and forks.

'Oh, I know. The obvious place would be' – I walked into my bedroom – 'in my sock drawer!' I pulled it open to find the pile of gleaming cutlery lying there innocently.

I chuckled as I walked back. Dan was standing in the kitchen holding up a grey wool sock, looking bemused.

'Dad,' I explained, not needing to say anything more.

Dan grinned, and nodded his understanding. He took one of the knives from my outstretched hand then opened the fridge door to find his vegan margarine. (Most of my staff eschewed animal products. People who passionately care about animals often choose to eat only plant-based food, but I'm afraid I have never been one of them. I am a bit old-fashioned, and the thought of living without my Sunday roast would be too much to bear. My staff didn't seem to mind, and apart from the occasional dig to try and convert me, they left me alone to enjoy my occasional meat dinner.)

That wasn't the only jest Dad played on me. Often, I'd walk into a room and screw up my eyes, wondering why it all looked wrong, then I'd realise that all the pictures were turned around to face the wall, or he'd deliberately put the frames all at jaunty angles so I felt like I was at sea. Silly things, some might say childish pranks, but they were all good-natured and made my father happy so I left him to it. He had always had funny little ways, and over the years that had never changed.

I watched him as he whistled a tune to himself, content to be sitting with me and Princess, and my heart swelled with love for him. For all his kind ways, he was a stubborn man, and I knew I'd have my work cut out to convince him to come and live inside the bungalow, though I'd decided that's what must happen. I had inherited this particular character trait, and so I knew how best to handle him: slowly and softly.

I made a mental note to start building an extension straight away. I wanted to make him a space that was joined onto the house with his own bedroom, bathroom and shower so I could keep a closer eye on him, and be reassured that he was warm and well fed. I'd have to tell him soon that he couldn't stay living in the old, now-rusty metal caravan, which was perishing cold in winter and stiflingly hot in summer, but for now, there was no point arguing.

'Okay Dad, whatever you want,' I murmured.

EIGHT

First Struggles

Getting Princess to learn to walk again had become my mission. She'd been with us for three weeks now, and it was time to make teaching her to walk again the top priority.

Even though there was always too much to do at the sanctuary, I'd explained to Diane and Dan that I would be devoting my time to helping Princess recover from the shock of the amputation, no matter how long it took. Both of them had been understanding, knowing how important Princess was to me, though Dan had asked if we could get a new worker to help him while I was engaged with the dog.

To my relief, we'd received a bequest a few days earlier, which had provided a much-needed boost to our finances. The unexpected extra money meant we could take on a paid employee and have enough to rebuild the cattery hospital, as Di had requested. I told Dan to put the word out among his wide circle of animal-loving friends and find someone to step in and help out.

Diane was keen to manage my expectations.

'You can't expect too much from Princess, Barby. Having a limb amputated is extremely stressful for any animal. It can take up to three weeks for a well-nourished, happy dog to recover from an operation like this, and it's clear that Princess wasn't either of those things before she arrived with us. Recovery time for her will naturally be longer, especially given the infection.'

Di knew pretty much everything about everything and she was a mine of information. Many times over the years I'd called on her expertise, and always appreciated her opinion.

'How long before she came to us do you think she had the operation?' I mused.

Di looked over at the pup. 'Probably a week or so, long enough time for the wound to become infected anyway.'

'Poor lamb. What else can we do to help her recover?' I asked.

'Most pets would adjust easily, especially if they'd been in pain for a long time as it would be a relief to them not to have that hurt. Princess has had a difficult start in life so ultimately it's going to be patience that you need, Barby, in spades.'

I chuckled at that. When it came to people, I had little or no patience, but when it came to dogs, it was another matter altogether.

As I thought about what Di had said, Princess cocked her funny little head and snuffled, wagging the whole bottom half of her body and standing up on her one front leg, the back legs remaining resolutely sitting.

'We'll get you there, little one,' I cooed as I bent down to pet her.

'She's got to get used to moving around in a different way. Most dogs I've seen that have this surgery recover well. Normal movement is going to feel strange to her, but once she learns to redistribute her weight onto the other three legs, she'll be bouncing about like a happy puppy in no time,' Di reassured me, beaming down at the little dog.

She was an optimist, always cheerful, always steady. She was my rock in many ways. While I was the spirited, impatient, feisty soul of the sanctuary, Diane was its steady, beating heart. We couldn't function without her. Her wisdom and calm were an integral part of our shelter, and I needed that more than ever with this dog.

'She can't jump up as she won't have enough strength in her remaining limbs, so you're doing the right thing in keeping her tucked up, though she will need to slowly build up the other limbs. She'll have lost a lot of muscle,' Di added, her face grim.

'The only good thing about her lack of mobility has been her weight gain. She still wolfs down everything I put in front of her, and begs for more all the time,' I told her.

'A sure sign of a starved animal,' Di chipped in.

'I don't think she was starved, but she was definitely not fed as well as she should have been,' I replied.

I sat down on the sofa next to Princess. I'd made her a nice bed on there, with water close by and lots of toys to amuse her. Already, Princess's confidence had grown dramatically. When she first came, she was almost silent and very hesitant about being stroked, but now she lapped up the affection, snuffling up to whoever sat next to her, man or woman, to be tickled and petted.

'She'll get there, Barby. But perhaps you might need to help her stand up yourself. I mean, actually hold on to her and give her a chance to put her weight down on her legs. I think you're going to have to do something, otherwise she'll end up staying like that.'

Di gently shook her head. She hated seeing a naturally friendly, playful pup acting like an invalid. She was right – it was time to push Princess a little, take her out of her comfort zone.

Dan was nodding in agreement. He hadn't said much, but he never usually dealt with the kennels or the dogs directly. His job was to manage and care for the farm animals, the cows, goats, donkeys, horses and sheep.

A day or so later, I bumped into Dan as he was making himself breakfast in the kitchen. 'Any luck with getting someone to help us out?' I asked.

'As it happens, I think we have had some luck. A guy called Fran has been working in a cat shelter in Sussex but wants to move on to something new. One of the volunteers knows him and so gave him a call yesterday. He's coming here next week. He's got loads of experience with horses, as well as dogs and cats, so I think he'll fit right in. He was a hunt saboteur in his day. Doesn't bother you, does it?' Dan asked, a smile playing on his lips.

Most of my volunteers had dabbled in animal activism at some point in their lives, so to exclude someone on this basis would've been foolish, even if I wasn't fully in agreement with their methods.

'As long as he isn't doing it now, I don't care,' I said stoutly.

Dan nodded again, and gave a laugh as he left. I didn't know what that meant, and I chose not to ask. I knew Dan had dabbled too, though he'd subsequently given it up. In the end, what I didn't ask, I didn't regret, so I let him go without further enquiry.

'You're number one on my list now, Princess,' I said, feeling the new fleshy belly covering her ribcage. 'You're looking podgier, which is a good thing for a pup. Good girl, Princess, you're doing amazingly well. Now we just need to take you to the next level, but I'm afraid it might not be easy . . .'

Princess licked my hand, bending her head round to sniff again at the missing leg. It looked like her way of understanding that what was there before had disappeared. She rolled onto her back, her three legs in the air as I scratched the smooth fur. Her skin wasn't flaking any more as it had been when she arrived, and she had meat on her bones.

Things were looking up for Princess, but she had to walk, and there was no time like the present to start.

I picked her up carefully. Princess made a little whining noise but I shushed her and carried on.

'Now then, I'm going to hold you up like this – that's it, put your legs down. We're going to stand like this for a few seconds and get you used to being upright again.'

Princess started to struggle, which I took as a good sign that she had some fight in her. I pulled myself round so that her face was in front of mine and I sat on the floor while I held her up. She licked my nose and her tail wagged, which made her wobble over to the right. It was her front left leg that had been cut off, and so all her weight toppled over towards me as soon as her tail started to move. I had to laugh. She looked so comical, her face appearing to hang down as she licked me again while trying to steady herself. After a while my arms grew tired so I gently helped her back down and into her bed, but I felt a surge of pride in her. It wasn't a big leap forward, but it was a start, her first struggles towards becoming a happy, playful dog again.

We tried this trick every day for a week. Even though the changes in Princess were minuscule, every day I thought I noticed a change. She stood for longer each time I held her up and I'd even started to let go and let her stand by herself, though she seemed to topple to the floor almost immediately at first. After a few days, though, she didn't appear to notice that I'd taken my hands away.

'Progress!' I said in delight after a particularly rewarding session. Princess had managed to stay upright for several minutes, but cried a little, though it seemed to be more out of confusion than pain.

'Well done, Princess!' cried Diane as she entered my lounge, plonking herself down onto the leather armchair where she always sat.

'We've just had a telephone call. A chihuahua is coming in today. Don't know the history but I think the couple can't afford to keep him any more,' she continued.

'Oh, that's awful, what a shame for them. It feels as though we're starting see this situation more and more often,' I sighed. 'It must be heartbreaking to lose your pet because you can't pay the bills. I can't think of anything worse.'

Diane and I shared a look. Was it our imagination, or were times becoming harder for people? We heard this same story over and over again. Benefits had been cut and people could no longer afford their beloved animals. Working hours had been reduced or cut completely, and people faced losing their homes, and everything that went with it, including their pets.

'What time is he coming in?' I asked, stroking Princess absent-mindedly.

'They're on their way now. Won't be more than ten minutes, I'd say,' Di said. 'Enough time for a quick cuppa.'

A couple of minutes later, Di walked in with my tea, steeped in sugar, just the way I liked it.

'It used to be that people left animals because they had to move, or because they couldn't look after them properly. Perhaps they had behavioural problems, or perhaps the owners became ill or infirm. We rarely saw people who couldn't afford to feed a pet,' Di continued, sighing.

'It's a scandal.' It was all I could say. I didn't understand why society seemed a harsher place for both people and animals.

Just then, the bell at the entrance to the sanctuary clanged loudly.

'Oh, here we go, they've arrived. Bring them in here, dear, will you? I want to stay close to Princess. I don't like leaving her on her own,' I said.

Diane went to greet the couple and returned a few moments later. Behind her followed a young couple, clearly very upset about leaving the little dog the man had in his arms.

They were both wearing jeans and trainers that had clearly seen better days and looked like they were struggling for money. As they talked, they explained that they also had a young daughter, who they'd left with her grandparents as it was too distressing for her to say goodbye to the dog. It was as upsetting a rehoming as I'd ever seen.

'He's a sweet little thing,' I said. 'We'll take care of him and find him a loving, permanent home where he'll be well looked after. You do have a week to think it over, though. If at the end of the seven days, you decide to come and get him, that'll be no problem at all,' I said, trying desperately to reassure them.

The young woman, whose name was Carrie, broke down as she had a last cuddle with the dog, crying softly as she stroked his soft fur.

The man, named Chris, was worse. He sobbed as he held the dog.

'He's only six months old. I would never have dreamed of giving him up, but my contract ended and I haven't found more work yet. We've tried, we've really tried to keep it all together . . .' He was clearly devastated, and my heart went out to them both. It was so unfair.

'Give him to me,' I said, gently, 'it's for the best. What's his name?' I asked as I held my arms out to Chris.

'He's called Robbie, or Rob,' he replied as he took a last look at the chihuahua then handed the small bundle over to me. The dog was a short coat breed with honey-coloured fur and big black eyes that peered out of his tiny face. Instantly he started to yap, struggling in my arms and trying to get back to his owners. I carried him out into the kitchen, and Di took the cue to take the couple into the office to fill out the forms. In our long years of experience, we knew that lengthy goodbyes only upset those involved even more.

Being a foster carer for unwanted animals was never going to be anything other than an emotional rollercoaster. I often thought I couldn't go on, couldn't bear to see so much suffering. I witnessed cruelties, neglect and abuse towards the animals that were left here, but in some ways this case was worse because these people clearly loved their dog desperately, but just couldn't afford to keep him because of circumstances beyond their control.

The tiny animal was quivering in my arms, and was clearly distressed.

'It's for the best,' I said again, this time to the dog, holding him close. 'Your breed is not great with small children anyway. You're not the most patient of dogs, and I've known chihuahuas attack their owners' babies, so I think you're probably in the right place.'

There had been no suggestion that this loud little fella was aggressive, but for all their size, these types of dogs were easily frightened and could attack the source of their fear, including small children.

He continued to yap. Even when I put him down on my bed, he continued to bark in sharp yips that made my ears hurt.

'I wonder if your noise was part of the reason they had to bring you to us?' I chuckled. 'I can't believe it, you're a dear little thing but you do yap a lot.'

The chihuahua was now running about in circles, sniffing the carpet and rugs and generally exploring his surroundings. He didn't seem so distressed now at his owner's departure. I'd heard the door being shut, and the sound of everyone leaving, including Diane. Suddenly struck by an idea, I picked up the young dog again and carried him, squirming, into the lounge.

I couldn't have said where the idea came from. Usually, I'd keep a new dog separate from any other canines in order to settle them in, and ease any companion dogs into their relationship together. This was different, though. It was the first time I'd ever done what I was about to do, and I had no idea if it would work or not. I carried the small dog into the lounge and placed him down close to Princess. Then I stood back and watched to see what would happen.

Instantly the chihuahua rushed straight to Princess's side, sniffing her tail, snuffling his nose, his perky little tail high behind him. The small dog's ears looked enormous in comparison to the size of his head and they were pricked up as if he was asking, 'What do we have here?'.

Princess responded enthusiastically. She sniffed in return and her tail, longer than the chihuahua's, wagged furiously. I held my breath, knowing that I was taking a risk. The chihuahua could easily find something he didn't like about Princess and react disproportionately. This breed was known for its tiny stature and its huge personality, yet as I watched, I had a feeling that all would be well. Princess rolled onto her back in submission, and mock play. Then she did something that made me gasp. She raised himself up on her remaining front leg and sat upright, looking at the new arrival.

'Princess! You're sitting up by yourself!' I exclaimed, clapping my hands with glee. Princess was wobbling and swaying slightly from side to side as she found her balance, but she'd done the impossible: she'd raised himself up using her only front leg. This was a huge step forward.

The tiny canine yapped and jumped about in response, ready for the play he was sure would follow.

When Princess didn't move any further, instead of wandering off, Rob sat himself down next to the puppy so their coats were touching. He was still barking away, even though the two of them appeared to have bonded imme-diately, and I saw that the minuscule dog, with his perky tail, huge ears, shining eyes and bouncy nature, seemed to be protecting Princess, peering round as if to announce: 'This is my new friend, I'll look after her.'

'Crikey, you can hear that dog barking from outside the house!' Di laughed as she came in.

Suddenly another idea came to me. I said affectionately, 'I'm going to call you Sonic Gob because you are the loudest little creature I've ever come across. It isn't too different from your name. Gob at least rhymes with Rob. How do you like that?' I crooned, holding my hand out for the excitable little chap to sniff.

At that moment, Harry sauntered in and slumped down on a rug by the fire. He had generally avoided being in the same room as Princess, preferring to sulk on my bed or trot outside rather than interact with the puppy that had stolen my affection, though not entirely. However, this new addition to the sanctuary had obviously piqued his interest, and he had come to find out more. Harry looked down at Sonic Gob as if to register his arrival, then flopped down on the rug by the fire, sniffing loudly and turning his head away.

'You really are the most grumpy dog I have ever come across,' I said. 'I know you're jealous of all these new pups but I still love you, even if you do sulk a lot.'

Harry looked over to me with reproachful eyes, which only made me chuckle.

'Poor Harry. He hasn't fallen for your noisy charms, Sonic, nor yours, Princess. What shall we do with him?'

In response, Sonic started yapping again, spinning round and round on the carpet, chasing his tail. Within minutes Harry shot me another reproachful look and slunk off into my bedroom, leaving me, the loquacious new dog and the puppy with three legs.

NINE

Starting to Limp

The void that Teddy left was always with me. The silly old Irish wolfhound had been my best friend, always at my side. I never had to look for him or wonder where he was because he was always within grasping distance. Over the past few months, I'd had days where I thought I couldn't cope without him, and even though Princess had appeared and needed much of my time and attention, the hole that Teddy had left was too big to fill.

Sometimes, like today, a brisk autumnal morning, I had a sense of him still, sitting by my side, his wiry fur ruffled by the wind that was blowing across our land. As I chatted to Dan and the other volunteers as we began work repairing the cattery hospital and extending it, I could have sworn I felt his bulky body lean against me, and I almost reached down to stroke his black straggly beloved head, though he wasn't there. He'd never be 'there' again.

'Barby . . . Barby, you there?' Dad asked, interrupting my memories. I looked up, and saw that Dan had been trying to get my attention. Now that we had the money, the work had also started to rebuild the cattery, and even though Dad was looking frail and very elderly, he was part of the team, and always seemed to be pottering around in the thick of the action as volunteers carried bags of cement in wheelbarrows, sawed pieces of wood or simply sipped tea and watched.

'Sorry, Dan,' I called to my farm manager, 'I was miles away. What do you need?'

A gust of the September wind almost blew Dan's woolly hat off as he leaned back off the ladder propped against the cattery wall.

'Watch what you're doing!' I shouted, 'I don't want to spend the day in A&E!'

Dan grinned. 'You worry too much, Barby. We need to know where you want the cats' areas – did you want them to go off to the side or to run parallel to the others?'

Looking straight ahead at the building, which was under-going its renovations, the area for older cats, the VIP area, was situated to the right of the hospital, while the actual pens for the cats, which were one storey-high enclosures fenced off with chicken wire, ran along the path leading to the doorway.

'Well, whatever happens, we need more enclosures. At the moment we're getting six cats in every day, and we're running out of space. I think we need to build a new row and it would make sense for them to sit parallel to the others so the cats can see each other.

'We could put chairs and tables out to make a nice seating area for visitors and plant up parts of the cattery between the rows, which will make it look pretty for all the prospective new owners.'

Dan nodded.

Another head poked round the side of the building.

'Hi, Dan, do you need a hand?' A man emerged who looked to be his early thirties, wearing the same scruffy work uniform as Dan, with jeans that looked encrusted with dirt, big working boots and an army cap.

'Oh, Barby, meet Fran. He started work here today,' Dan called out from the ladder.

'Hello, Fran.' I smiled, walking over to shake his hand. 'And where have you come from?' I liked to know the people who worked on my site.

'Nice to meet you, Barby. I was at a cat sanctuary and before that, well you probably don't want to know,' the new guy replied, making Dan snort with laughter.

'So, you were one of those hunt saboteur types, were you?' I frowned, hoping I looked as fierce as I sounded as I glared between him and Dan. I knew what they were alluding to; I wasn't such a daft old bat. I still had a good head on my shoulders and I could sniff out a fib at a hundred paces.

However, I also wanted to get our meeting off to a good start, and by that I mean letting him know who was in charge. While I understood why people would want to be involved with animal activism, I didn't want any illicit behaviour while they worked for me. I had to set the tone and let him know who was boss, stamping my authority on the situation. I didn't want any funny business on my land.

Unfortunately, Fran appeared to see right through me.

'Ha, and the rest,' he laughed, pulling his cap round so I could see his face more clearly. His eyes twinkled with merriment, and I saw it was useless to try and have any sway over him. This man was most definitely a character.

'I'm still in touch with loads of hunt sabs, though I don't do it any more. Doesn't mean I don't keep in touch though,' Fran said conversationally. I couldn't believe how candid he was being.

'You do understand, *don't you*, that none of that goes on while you're working for me?' I said, emphasising my words as I was speaking them.

'Course I do. I'm not stupid – you'll see,' he laughed before sauntering around the corner and starting to haul up a load of wooden planks to Dan.

I watched them for a moment. He and Dan got on, that much was obvious, but I wasn't sure yet about the newcomer. He seemed too confident in himself somehow, too relaxed perhaps.

Hmm, I said to myself, *I'll need to keep an eye on that one.*

'Barby, oh there you are,' Diane's voice sounded behind me.

I turned to see her running over to me, looking quite out of breath.

'You've got to come and see this,' she panted.

'See what?' I returned in bemusement. What could be so urgent to stop me overseeing the build?

'Just come. You'll find out for yourself.'

I cocked an eyebrow at this but I was intrigued.

'Dan, I'm going back to the house for a few moments. Will you be okay?' I shot over my shoulder, already taking the first steps in the direction of my house.

'Course we will, Barby!' Dan's indignant voice shouted back at me.

'Alright, Di, what is it? I'm coming.' I followed her back.

She looked excited, almost giddy even. Whatever it was, it was clearly something good.

I trotted behind her back to the house. As we opened the front door, the familiar sound of Sonic Gob's incessant barking greeted us.

'He's at it again. Does that dog ever stop yapping?' I said, sighing in mock exasperation. I've never worried about a dog barking. I have infinite patience with canine peculiarities, but as I've said, I have very little when it comes to humans. If a person was talking at me all day, every day, I'd probably throw something at them. When it came to Sonic, I just tuned it out, simply putting it down to his character.

'Come this way and see what they're doing. Oh, I hope they're still playing,' Di chatted as I walked behind her. We arrived at the lounge. Di stepped aside to let me in first, and the sight that greeted me made my heart sing.

Sonic and Princess were playing on the floor, rolling about, happy as anything. Princess seemed to have forgotten that she had a missing leg, and though she wasn't walking or standing up, she was rolling and shuffling herself about with complete abandonment.

Both dogs barked and yipped as part of their play-fighting, a sight that always brings great happiness to me. Two dogs enjoying each other's company and playing together is a marvel to see.

'Oh, look at them. They're so happy. Oh, what good dogs!' I cried, clapping my hands together in glee.

I crouched down and watched them closely. Sonic was now pretending to growl at Princess as Princess lay on the floor, her tail twitching, her large right front paw held up as if she really was going to box her friend.

'They're playing . . . they're really playing. Oh, how wonderful!'

I was gobsmacked. Sonic had somehow brought Princess out of herself, and just as quickly as Sonic had appeared in our lives, he'd brought about a transformation in the puppy.

Princess made her own growling noises with the occa-sional bark. She pretended to bite and chew at Sonic, while the chihuahua jumped and nipped at her.

Then, Sonic jumped away, and before our eyes, Princess struggled up, her front paw splayed out, her back legs straightening to support her.

Both Di and I held our breath. Could this really be happening? What I had failed to make Princess do voluntarily over the past few weeks, Sonic was about to accomplish in an afternoon of play.

Princess was standing, wobbling dangerously as she stood, but she was trying desperately hard to balance as Sonic bounded around the room. Princess tried to put her foot forward but at that point she came crashing down onto the rug. I gasped, but Princess didn't seem phased. In fact, within seconds she was trying to get up again.

I couldn't hold my excitement in any longer. I dashed over and helped her up, holding her steady so she could bark at Sonic like a 'proper' dog.

'Go, Princess, go on, give him hell,' I laughed, feeling tears prick my eyes. I was so proud of her. She'd been utterly traumatised, subjected to unknown cruelties and the horrors of poorly executed surgery. She was a little miracle, and now she was standing, trembling with the effort but trying with all her strength to remain upright. I couldn't have been happier, even if Teddy had walked back into that room.

Princess didn't last long in her standing position, but that wasn't the point. The point was that she was trying, and that was all we could ask of her.

After the game finished, both dogs flopped down onto Princess's rug to pant and doze for the rest of the afternoon.

I didn't go back out to the cattery. I wanted to stay indoors with the dogs and take in what had happened. I lifted the puppy onto my lap and she greeted me like an old friend. She licked my cheek and chin while I pretended that I didn't like it, exclaiming, 'Stop that, horrible dog,' which made her tail wag even harder.

She settled down and slept as I went through the admin papers that had begun to pile up on my desk. Things were moving forward. One day, if Princess carried on improving, we might even be able to rehome her. It wasn't a thought I relished, though. I'd very quickly become attached to the beautiful boxer snoozing contentedly in my lap. It was impossible not to be. Her eyes were so doleful, her expression so sweet, as though she was listening to every word I said, and I'd quite fallen in love with her. However, I knew that we should do our job and find her a new home, one where her disability was given round-the-clock attention, somewhere she could live out her days in happiness and harmony. I had briefly given thought to her staying here but my heart was still too broken from Teddy's death. I knew I couldn't give her all the love she deserved, and I was so busy with the day-to-day running of the sanctuary that I couldn't give her as much attention as she needed either.

*

Later, Di and I were sitting in the lounge at the end of the day as the fire crackled in the hearth and we sipped tea and chatted about the day.

Princess was asleep by the fire with Sonic's small body curled against her protectively.

'What a funny sight they are,' exclaimed Diane.

'Aren't they just,' I replied, stirring my hot drink and munching on a Hobnob.

'Have you given any more thought to Princess's future?' Diane asked. Sometimes I thought she must be a mind-reader. How did she know I was preoccupied with that very idea?

'Well yes I have, to be honest. I think it's time she moved to the kennels. Dan tells me there's space, and, if I'm honest, I don't want to get too attached to her. I couldn't face losing another dog, even though we've only known Princess for a few weeks. She's such a dear little thing that it would be easy to love her enough to want to keep her.' I knew I could speak my mind and be honest with Di.

She looked at me, taking in everything I was saying, then nodded as I finished.

'I wondered if having Princess in the house would be too much for you, so soon after losing Ted . . .' It wasn't often Di mentioned my beloved's dog's name. She had been as besotted with him as me; in fact, everyone on site had a soft spot for the lovable beast who knocked everything flying with one wag of his big tail, and came up almost to my chest in height.

He had left a big gap for all of us, and, in a way, I didn't want to fill it. In my grief, I felt as though I needed to keep that gap for Teddy, at least for the time being.

'I think moving her to the kennel so she can be looked after by a wider group of people is a good idea. Fran is very good with the dogs and he's got years of experience with animals of all kinds. I think it's safe to leave Princess in his hands as well as all the others,' Di continued. She sipped her tea and smiled at me.

'Okay, well in that case she can be moved tomorrow. She must have her blankets with her so she feels safe, though, and Sonic must go with her. They must be either in the same kennel, or in adjoining ones,' I replied, my voice shaking a little. I had grown *very* fond of both little critters.

'Of course, Barby,' replied Di calmly. She didn't dare look at me. If she had, I may have had to turn away. I could feel tears welling at the corners of my eyes and that familiar soreness that revealed how many I'd shed in the months previously.

'She'll be absolutely fine, they know what they're doing,' said Di reassuringly.

I knew she was right, but I had to admit that I'd miss having the comical pup around.

The next day, I was as good as my word, and after breakfast I reached for my walkie-talkie. Every key member of staff had one. It was easier and quicker than using different mobile telephones.

'Dan, are you there?' I said into the mouthpiece.

The handset buzzed.

'What do you want, Barby?' Dan had put on his best 'exasperated with Barby' voice.

'Well none of your cheek for starters!' I countered. 'Princess is coming over to the kennels. Would you make sure her new home is cosy, please?'

'Fran will take her, I'm busy.' And with that, the walkie-talkie crackled then went silent.

'Cheeky blighter,' I exclaimed.

I looked over at the dog. I was about to bring her her breakfast as I usually did when a thought occurred to me.

'Alright, Princess, let's see how you manage if I leave your bowl over here. Come on, girl, it's time for you to *walk* over to your food. Can you do that?'

Sonic bounded over as I put his bowl on the floor. He started eating greedily, while the puppy looked at us both, almost a look of astonishment on her face.

'Come on, I know you can do it. Come on, Princess, come and have your breakfast.'

Then, just as I was about to give up on her, Princess stood up. She actually stood up by herself, and then with shaking limbs and trembling paws, she limped forward, moving her back legs forward first, then her front paw followed. One step. Then another. She limped slowly, with fierce determination, towards her bowl.

'Good girl, oh you absolute beauty. Come on, you deserve this.' I placed the bowl on the floor next to Sonic's, making sure the noisy chihuahua didn't try to eat his friend's food.

After several, wobbly steps, Princess made it at last. I couldn't believe it. She'd walked for the first time since she'd been abandoned here at the sanctuary and I could have wept with joy. Instead, I crouched down next to her and stroked down her back, feeling the shivering in her weakened body subsiding.

After the two dogs had finished their food, I picked up Princess. It would've been too much to expect her to try to walk to the kennels.

'Come on, Sonic Gob, let's take you both over,' I said as I grabbed the puppy's blankets and together we walked out of my house and across the yard, veering left before reaching the shelter entrance to the kennels, which sat to the south-east of my house.

The block was new and had a row of six pens, with an extra for emergency or overnight admissions.

Four of the sections were occupied, and as we approached, the dogs, all Staffordshire bull terriers, began to bark then howl, thinking they were being fed or going for a walk.

'Sorry, you noisy mutts, this isn't your walkies time. The volunteers will arrive soon,' I said in a sing-song voice.

Sonic trotted obediently at my heels as he would be living in the pen next door to Princess. I had toyed with the idea of putting them in the same pen so that they remained together, but I thought it best if Princess was given her own space to recover in her own time. Every day, I would bring the funny pair over to the house first thing in the morning, then return them 'home' at night, so they would still be able to play together.

'Is that the puppy with just three legs?' Fran was leaning against the doorway, chatting to one of the young female volunteers. I raised my eyebrows at him and he gave me a cheeky smile.

'Shouldn't you be working?' I said icily, which made him laugh out loud.

'It's half past six, Barby, I've been here all night. We had a Staffie come in at 2 a.m. He'd been picked up wandering on a motorway by a motorist. He was lucky to be alive, and lucky that he didn't cause a pile-up.' Fran didn't ever seem to take offence. To my surprise, I realised I was starting to quite like him.

'Fancy a cup of tea?' he added, winking at me. 'Best cup of tea you'll ever have in your life.'

I snorted my response then handed Princess to him.

'Here, take her off me. I'll want to keep her if you don't.' I shrugged.

Fran nodded. 'Do you take sugar?'

He took me in his stride. Yes, I'd started to like him a lot.

'Four, and don't scrimp on the teaspoons,' I answered as I watched him place Princess carefully into her bed area. Sonic Gob was already jumping around his pen, throwing stuffed toys in the air and barking with that insistent yapping that was starting to drive everyone mad at the house.

'Don't worry about Princess, Barby. She's already at home. She'll be watched night and day,' Fran said, handing me a cup of tea. I sipped it and almost spat out the hot liquid.

'Ah, I've given you mine. Here's your diabetes overload,' joked Fran.

'How can you drink it like that?' I laughed.

'I'm sweet enough,' said Fran.

We both turned to look at the dogs I was leaving to his care. Sonic was snuggled up against the wire mesh that separated the pens, with Princess curled up against him.

'And so are they,' I added.

TEN

Shocking Events

Every morning after that, I would head down to the kennels as soon as I was washed and dressed. Most days I would greet Fran or whoever was with Princess, before picking the little dog up and carrying her back to mine. Sonic would trot after me, and I would spend the early hours playing with them both, encouraging the puppy to walk in the funny way she'd developed, half limping, half shuffling herself forward, in an effort to build up the muscles in her legs, and learn to regain her balance.

I knew I was neglecting my duties at the sanctuary, but something about her plight had touched me to the core. I knew very well how it felt to be neglected and unloved, just as Princess had been. Her rejection by her owner had reminded me of the deep pain I still carried from my child-hood. As I have mentioned, I grew up watching my mother adore my brother Peter. He was the golden child of our family. He had blonde hair and a sunny smile and was always cheerful, always full of fun and giggles, whereas I was a small, scrawny, brown-haired child with a permanent scowl and a constant case of the grumps. I don't know if I came into the world that way, or whether seeing all of my mum's love directed towards my brother made me sour and sullen.

Mum would reprimand me for everything, or so it seemed to me. My hair would never be brushed properly, my face never scrubbed clean enough, my attitude never quite right, and so I retreated into myself, just as my father had done after years of marriage to her. I clung to my dad and spent all the hours I wasn't doing chores for Mum sitting with him while we cared for whichever creature he'd brought home. I spent many a happy hour perched on his knee stroking an abandoned kitten, nursing a hedgehog with a poorly foot or helping to hold a puppy still while Dad brushed its matted fur. Mum would stand at the doorway, hands on her hips, her face set in a permanent grimace as she surveyed me and Dad. She would tut loudly and slam doors to make her displeasure known, but Dad and I never gave up saving the animals that followed him home like a real-life Pied Piper.

I knew she didn't love me. I knew I was a burden to her, whereas my brother was a delight. She cuddled and kissed him, kept the best cuts of meat for him, praised him for everything, sat reading with him each evening, while I burned with longing for a kind word or a hug. I don't ever remember my mother touching me with affection. I didn't receive any kisses or cuddles. I wasn't spoken to softly or caringly, except by Dad. In short, I was an unhappy child and I left home as soon as possible.

Despite all this, I adored Peter. I had never resented him for the love our mother showed only to him, even though it caused me so much pain. He was the centre of my world. I looked up to him and would wait for him to come home from school, my nose pressed up against the window, making my mother tut even more as I always left a smear where my nose had been. Ironically, he was the only one who understood how our mother was with me, and he tried to come between Mum and me on many occasions, and although his interventions often managed to diffuse the tension, he could never truly eradicate it.

Every time I looked at Princess, I saw another rejected, unwanted baby, though unlike Princess, I had been cared for physically. I had always been given clean clothes, good shoes and a full tummy. Mother never neglected my physical needs, and that, at least, I was grateful for. It looked like Princess hadn't been so lucky. Part of the reason I became so emotionally attached to the animals that were dumped here was because I felt an affinity with them.

'That's it, Princess, up you get.' My thoughts were interrupted by the sight of the three-legged pup standing up and limping after Sonic, who was pretending to growl at her fiercely. It was a Sunday morning and it had now been five months since Princess had arrived with us. With the help of her firm friend Sonic, the little boxer was now fairly mobile, although the bottom shuffle limp she'd developed to move herself around hadn't changed much in spite of the many hours I'd spent tempting her with treats, holding her and placing her front leg forward to encourage her to learn how to walk again.

With each month that passed, Princess, who was now six months old, had grown bigger and glossier as she was being fed properly, but her mobility continued to be a concern. Meanwhile, Dad had been installed into the new extension, which Dan and the guys had erected with little fuss over the previous winter. The sanctuary was closed to visitors between October and April each year to allow us to do any necessary rebuilding works, fence fixing or structural repairs. We continued to accept rescue animals during this time, and constantly strived to rehome the animals in our care – these were things that never closed. It meant we could fully concentrate on the site and our twelve acres, instead of hosting all the wonderful visitors who came each Sunday in the spring and summer seasons to eat cake, drink tea, buy plants and spend time with the animals.

In the end, much to my relief, Dad hadn't objected to being moved into the house. I'd sat him down one evening, intending to use all my persuasive powers to make the case for why he needed to leave behind the caravan and allow me to look after him more, but he'd patted my hand as we sat, and said, 'I know what this is all about, Barby. You think I didn't realise who that new extension is for? I'm not daft you know . . .'

I'd been feeling wretched about having this conversation, as I knew how independent my father was, yet we'd all seen his deterioration in recent months; how his hands shook these days; how forgetful he was becoming; how any exertion left him panting for breath.

It was ironic that as Princess's strength returned, my father's had waned.

Before I could respond, he said, in his quiet way, 'You want me to move in? Well, alright. I don't want to cause any trouble. If it makes you happier having me here then I'll move my stuff in today.'

I smiled, a sigh of relief escaping my lips.

'You certainly won't be moving your stuff,' I replied, squeezing his outstretched hand. 'The lads will do it for you. All you need to do is sit there and watch the others work. You've earned the right to rest now, Dad,' I said.

Dad nodded.

'Everything you need will be here, and I can keep an eye on you, keep you out of trouble.' I smiled, which made him chuckle.

I knew he would miss his caravan keenly. He'd lived inside it for twenty years through snow and gales, blistering summer heat through to drizzle and autumnal evenings. It would be a wrench for him to give up his independence but I knew everyone here would make it as easy as possible for him.

And so, Dad moved in. I had taken him to the doctor's to get him checked over, but the GP reassured us it was just old age, though I was concerned to see he was losing weight still and had seemed all the more fragile recently.

'That's it, Princess, you're almost running!' I said gleefully.

Princess limped after Sonic, who rolled over, faking his own capture. I could've watched them for hours but I had work to do. Our Summer Fair was the next big event we would undertake, after a successful Christmas Bazaar, and as it usually raised half of our annual funds, it was an important date in our diary. I had to start ringing round to ask local businesses to donate prizes for our raffle, there were stalls to organise, sponsors to call and transport to coordinate. I needed to make up time as I'd lost days caring for Princess and settling Dad.

I smiled over at the dogs. 'I've got work to do, you two – you've got to stop distracting me now. Go and play with my father. He's always happy to see you.'

Dad kept more and more to his rooms these days. Throughout his late eighties, he'd been as busy as anyone else, clearing out sheds, working in the cattery and gardening around the site, but he suddenly seemed tired, his ninety-six years weighing him down at long last. I worried about him constantly, but at least he was nearby and could receive the best possible care and attention.

Sonic grabbed a chew toy in the shape of a bone and sat down with it, guarding his precious treasure while Princess slumped down too. She had spurts of energy where she could limp after the smaller dog, but she tired quite easily, and I could see she was ready for a break. The bond between Princess and Sonic was extraordinary. Sonic always seemed to know when the pup needed to rest, and would automatically settle down next to her.

I eyed them both over my glasses, then picked up a pile of unopened letters, mostly from the vet, and started to leaf through them. I'd already been up at the cattery working that morning and I couldn't put off my admin any longer.

One letter stood out. It had PRIVATE AND CONFIDENTIAL stamped on the front.

'This doesn't look good,' I muttered to myself, opening the envelope and peeling out the letter. It was from Rother District Council serving a Noise Abatement Order on the sanctuary. I gasped and almost dropped the paper. I scanned the words again, this time more slowly to take it all in.

We'd had a few threats of court action by disgruntled owners in the past who had come back for the pets they'd signed away months ago, only to find they'd been rehomed. Nothing had ever come of these, but this was different. This was an actual order telling me that due to complaints about the dogs in the kennels barking too much, I was being prosecuted. A neighbour had claimed the barking of our rescue dogs was a disturbance.

I sat down heavily. I knew exactly who it was. A new couple had recently bought the house nearest the sanctuary, and I was stunned when, a few weeks after moving in, they came to complain about the noise. I had thought that they'd have realised that moving in next to an animal shelter would mean experiencing animal noises, but they were most disgruntled. I'd tried to explain as politely as I could that dogs bark to communicate, and when dogs are first rehomed or dumped at our door, it was understandable that they might've barked more than would be normal. They soon settled down as we cared for them. We only had six dogs in our kennels, and of course, they barked, but didn't all dogs? It wasn't as though I had a place full of them.

For a moment, I was so shocked I could hardly breathe, but the shock turned almost immediately to anger. If the council upheld this, it could mean that I wouldn't be able to rescue dogs any more. It would mean that ill or unwanted canines would have to be turned away. This couldn't happen. I vowed to myself, then and there, to do everything I could to fight this ridiculous order.

Immediately, I picked up the telephone and called a solicitor we had heard good things about.

'You can appeal, though I'm guessing the council will contest it,' he said.

'I don't care what the blimmim' council does. I will fight this all the way. How can they be so cruel as to stop me taking in dogs? It would mean I'd be forced to turn away animals that make a noise – and that's just madness,' I ranted.

'Try to stay calm, Ms Keel, and don't, whatever you do, go barging round to the people concerned and demand they retract it. You'll only make matters worse.'

He'd read my mind. I had half a mind to march over to the couple and bang on their door to demand what they were up to.

'The worst thing is, they've put the house up for sale so it looks like they're moving away anyway,' I said miserably. 'Why didn't they just speak to me properly, then none of this would have happened.'

'You don't know that, Barby. To make a case to the council means backing it up with proof. They will have spent time and trouble making this case against you. It's your job now to appeal and let the court decide,' he said.

'What will it mean for us, if the court does decide to uphold it?' I asked, my voice wavering a little. I felt suddenly tearful, the anger draining away from me, leaving me shocked and upset.

'If the order is upheld, and there will need to be strong evidence to do that, but if the worst comes to the worst, it could affect whether your planning permission for the sanctuary is renewed.'

I listened in silence. I had been angry before, but this made me feel scared. I felt a cold shiver down my back. This would indeed be the worst possible news.

'Do you mean that I could lose the sanctuary, in effect?' I asked in a trembling voice.

'Now, Barby, let's not talk about the worst-case scenario. I'm sure that you will have a robust defence, and it's best we confine ourselves to thinking about that. Try not to worry,' he said.

Try not to worry? Those words were meaningless to me – of course I'd worry!

But there was nothing else I could say.

'Thank you,' I muttered before hanging up the phone and picking up my walkie-talkie.

'Diane, would you let the trustees know that we need to have an emergency meeting? We have to mount a defence against this stupidity,' I said over the walkie-talkie.

'What stupidity?' Di replied. 'What's happened?'

'Just call a meeting please, dearest, and I'll explain everything.'

As I sat digesting this latest drama in the life of our sanctuary, I was struck by the sudden realisation that Dad hadn't emerged from his room that morning. I'd checked on him earlier and he'd been asleep in his chair, which was not entirely unusual for him, but I'd never known him sleep so late in the morning. It was almost ten o'clock, and he was usually up and about by seven at the latest.

Without another thought to our dilemma, I put the letter down and headed into my father's annexe, trying to calm the inexplicable rising of panic. *He'll be fine, he'll be fine*, I repeated to myself, but my gut was telling me that something was wrong, and every instinct pricked up like the boxer pup's ears. I felt like I was moving through treacle as I headed into his bedroom. It was like one of those dreams where you're being chased but you can't run away fast enough. I half ran, half walked into his room. He was in exactly the same position he'd been when I checked on him earlier, his head hanging down. But now, there appeared to be something terribly wrong with his face.

Dear God, he's had a stroke, I realised in a split second. I raced to him, checking his pulse. To my relief, he was alive and breathing but was unconscious. I became suddenly aware of my heart hammering, a cold feeling creeping through my body as I ran to the phone and dialled 999.

'It's urgent. My father, he's had a stroke. I checked him this morning. I should've known then, I should've known . . . He's at the animal sanctuary. Yes, that one, everyone knows us here.' I didn't know what I was gabbling to the operator.

As soon as I was assured the ambulance was on its way, I dashed back to his side, patting his hands, trying to hold him upright in the chair.

The minutes seemed to drag by. I buzzed Diane on the walkie-talkie.

'Come quickly,' I said, feeling a sob form in my throat.

'What? Why?' Di asked. 'Is it related to earlier?'

'No, just come. It's Dad. I think he's had a stroke,' I replied, my hand shaking as I held the mouthpiece.

'I'm on my way,' Di said firmly.

Within seconds she arrived, running through the door and into Dad's annexe.

'Have you—?'

I interrupted her before she could finish. 'Yes, I've rung for an ambulance. I think they knew where to come, though I'm not sure.'

I stared at her helplessly.

'Right, I'll go out to the lane and flag them down. Try not to panic, Barby. We'll all do the best we can for him.'

Diane ran off.

I turned back to Dad, who I was holding, whispering into his ear that we were all here, there was nothing to worry about, that he'd be fine. I had no idea if this was true or not.

Time passed excruciatingly slowly, but eventually there came the sound of the door opening, followed by Di's voice and hurried footsteps.

I stepped aside as the paramedics checked him over. The room seemed to blur and I realised I was in shock.

'I'm coming with him to the hospital,' I said firmly, in a voice that couldn't be argued with.

I don't remember the journey to the Irvine Unit in Bexhill where intensive care was based. I don't remember going into the hospital, entering the ward or any of the faces of the doctors who worked on Dad with an urgency I recognised as critical. All I remember are inconsequential details like the smell of the disinfectant on the ward, and the sound of machines beeping. My brain seemed to freeze with the shock of seeing my father lying there, almost lifeless.

I was there for what seemed like hours before Dad regained consciousness. He stirred, then his head came up a little and he peered around before saying, slowly, 'Get me out of here, it's full of old people.'

'You're alive. I was starting to wonder!' I joked even though I could've cried with relief.

'I'll get you out of here as soon as I can,' I promised him, reaching for his hand. His face was pale as he blinked at me. I felt my heart swoop down to my stomach. I knew I couldn't leave him there, all alone, overnight.

The next morning, the sound of the nurse doing the rounds woke me up. I stretched, my back aching and my head thick with lack of sleep. I'd stayed all night with Dad, dozing for a couple of hours at a time in the plastic chair next to his bedside.

'Sorry, Dad,' I murmured, 'I have to get back to the animals.' Dad was still sleeping, his face looking more peaceful in the early morning sunshine.

As I got up to leave, I walked to the nurses' station. The consultant had been around the ward the evening before and had said very little about Dad's condition except that he was stable. I hoped the nurses would give me more information.

'How long will he have to be in here?' I asked.

The matron, a kind-looking woman in her forties, turned to me, and said gently: 'Miss Keel, your father has had a stroke. We won't know for sure how he will recover, or even how much damage may have been done, for days, if not weeks. It may take a long time.'

I was silent for a moment, before replying, 'I want to care for him myself. When he's able to be taken home, I want you to let me know and I'll be here. We'll look after him, however poorly he may be.'

My face must have shown something of the fierce love I felt for him, because the matron smiled, put her hand on my arm, and said something I'll never forget. She said: 'What a wonderful daughter you are. So many people bring their elderly relatives in here and just leave them. Some never come back for them at all.'

'But he's my dad,' I said, as if it was the most obvious thing in the world. What I meant by that, of course, was 'I love him.'

ELEVEN

Learning to Move

'You there, Barby?' My father's reedy voice sounded from behind the curtain.

'Yes, it's me, Dad, how are you feeling?' I asked as I pulled aside the long blue material that separated my father from the only other patient in his small side room of the hospital ward.

My father's head turned as I entered, his face breaking into a slow smile.

'You took your time,' he chuckled, which made me grin.

'You're still in here, then?' I joked, sitting on the chair beside his bed and reaching for one of his hands. His skin felt papery thin, his veins blue and protruding as they ran snake-like across the top of it. What I meant, of course, was that he was seeming more and more like his old self, a fact that I found deeply reassuring.

My father had been in hospital for several weeks and little had changed in that time except he endured his daily physiotherapy sessions with his typical good grace. Dad was still visibly weak and could only shuffle a little while upright and supported by me or a nurse. He had lost his ability to keep his balance completely, and he complained of tingling sensations in his body. His memory had been affected badly too, and despite my relief to hear his trademark humour when he first regained consciousness, he seemed confused much of the time he was awake. He lapsed in and out of consciousness, but despite his state, I knew he would be better off at home. I made a mental note to speak to his team again, though I wouldn't mention it to my father until plans were more concrete, as his moods were variable, as were his levels of alertness and awareness.

He slipped in and out of consciousness. Some days, like today, he seemed almost the same as he ever was. He would recognise me, say hello and ask me to tell him what was happening at the sanctuary. Other days, he would lie slumped against his pillows, staring into space, and I'd wonder if he even knew I was there. On those occasions, I carried on chatting as usual, yet feeling like the father I adored was already lost to me. He was ninety-six years old, a great age by any standard, and I knew this was the beginning of the end, which is why I felt so determined to get him home.

Dad was next door to a little old man who, in the weeks since Dad had been in the hospital, being visited every day, hadn't had a single visitor.

'Hello, Bill,' I'd said to the man as I passed his bedside that morning. I felt so desperately sorry for him. In fact, I'd started a new routine during my long days on the ward. Whenever Dad fell asleep or was being entertained by the television, I would sit by Bill, chatting to him about the sanctuary and generally keeping him company. It was the only way I could square my conscience. I couldn't bear to ignore him, and leave him there all alone. If Di came in with me, or any one of the volunteers as they all loved my dad, I would make them sit with Bill, or take it in turns to visit Dad and the elderly man.

'You're too soft-hearted.' Dan said one evening upon my return to the sanctuary. I knew he didn't really mean it. He wouldn't have been able to let that man suffer alone either.

'It's a crying shame, Dan. He's had nobody, nobody at all, come in to see if he's okay. Why are people so cruel?'

'We ask ourselves that every day,' Dan said quietly.

For a moment there was silence as we both contemplated his words.

'And on that note, we've got a new horse in,' he said eventually, breaking the spell. 'She's called Betsy and she's got a deformed foot, though she isn't in pain.'

'What's her story?' I asked, yawning. I'd been with Dad during the morning and evening visiting hours and still had lots of work to catch up on, though perhaps I'd leave it for that night. I wasn't exactly a spring chicken myself these days, and I was starting to recognise that I couldn't do the same heavy lifting and dawn-till-dusk workload that I'd done all of my life. I was feeling tired more and more often, but I also knew that part of that was the shock of Dad's illness, as well as the stress of the court case, which was now looming. My appeal against the Noise Abatement Order was to be held in May, a couple of weeks away, at Hastings Magistrates' Court. I was dreading it, and all the worrying had combined to leave me unable to sleep.

Dan shrugged. 'She was just unwanted.'

I nodded. It was a story we heard time and time again. Animals were simply left. Their owners either moved, or decided they were too expensive to keep, or vanished into thin air. Betsy was just one of many.

'Did you submit all the Defra forms?' I yawned again, more loudly this time.

'Of course, Barby. Why don't you get some rest? If there's anything that needs doing, we'll sort it. Princess has had a great day playing with Sonic, and she seems able to get pretty much anywhere on her three legs. One of the volunteers took her down to Bexhill beach today while you were with your dad. She loved the sea though struggled on the pebbles.'

I felt guilty. I hadn't even asked about Princess, and I definitely hadn't been able to give the dog any of my time or attention for weeks now.

'I'll take her out for a walk around the site tomorrow. Perhaps we'll visit Betsy and see how she's settling in,' I said. 'Goodnight, Dan.'

'Goodnight, Battleaxe. Don't let the bastards grind you down!'

I had to laugh at that. Although there were days when I felt completely ground down, I had to be grateful for the wonderful army of staff and helpers I worked with, who at times like this kept both me and the sanctuary going.

The next day, I told Princess that we would have a little shuffle around the land together. I wanted to visit the piglets, which were already quite large, and growing fatter by the day by all accounts.

Di had arranged to go and sit with Dad for the day to give me a break. I didn't need to put Princess on a lead as she never moved fast enough, and so we set out to visit the sties via the horse enclosure. She was a little nervous when it became clear we weren't walking from the kennel back to the bungalow but going around the back, past the kennels and out into the neighbouring paddock. She held back a bit, sniffing the air, her funny little head cocked to the side, which was her trademark expression. Luckily, one of the jobs that had been done over the winter was the creation of a pathway leading down to the horses, and Princess managed the walk admirably.

'You're doing very well,' I said, reaching in my pocket

for a treat, which Princess almost snatched out of my hand. 'Hmmm, we might need to start working on your manners, though,' I laughed, patting her soft brown head.

It was a glorious spring morning. There were hardly any clouds in the blue sky; those that did hover overhead were white and wispy. The dew still lay on the grass and as we walked, that fresh smell of clean soil, grass and morning mist enveloped us.

Princess was managing to keep up with me with her funny, lopsided limp, though she struggled when we made it to the uneven ground.

I watched as she made her awkward way through the grass, knowing she would probably never be able to run and play like an able-bodied dog. The thought made me sad. Both Dad and Princess would never recover properly, my father because of his great age and fragility, the dog because of the amputation.

'At least you've got a long life ahead of you, Princess, whereas Dad . . .'

Princess was sitting down at my feet, her head on my lap as I sat on the grass. We had stopped for a break, and another dog biscuit. As soon as the words were out of my mouth, the terrible truth dawned on me at last. Dad wasn't ever going to recover from his stroke. This truly was the beginning of the end. I had to get him home as soon as possible so I could care for him in his last days. Tears came then, thick and hot on my cheeks. I attempted to wipe them away with a corner of my sleeve, and Princess, sensing my distress, quietly sat up, carefully veered over to the right and proceeded to lick the salt tears off my face.

'Stop, you daft mutt. I don't want to be kissed, no I don't . . .'

I cried and cried, Princess staying faithfully by my side, as the outpouring of truth, and the beginnings of grief, engulfed me.

When my body had stopped shaking from my sobs, I took a long, deep breath. From behind my red eyes, the sanctuary land looked the same and yet everything had changed. I looked down at Princess and kissed the soft fur on her sleek body, making her tail thump against the ground as she wagged it.

'We have to find a way to get you better. This is no condition for a young boxer. You should be leaping and jumping in the grass, chasing rabbits and sticks and haring through the undergrowth. There must be a solution, there just must.'

From nowhere, Fran appeared, whistling a tuneless melody as he sauntered across the grass.

'Oh, hello, Barby, I was wondering where you were. I'm checking in on Betsy. Apparently she's lame in one foot so I'm going to have a look at her,' he said. 'Want me to help you up?' This time he was grinning.

'No, I do not, thank you very much,' I said archly. He'd already realised in his short time with us how much I prickled at offers of help. Because of my childhood, I've always been a very self-contained, independent person, and find it hard to ask for help even if I'm desperate.

'Haha, I thought not. Come on then, you old hag, let's have a look at this horse.'

I had to smile. Not many people got away with calling me names these days, but I had warmed to Fran when I saw how gentle he was with the animals, and how irreverent he was with humans. I liked him, and I liked to have a banter as well.

'There aren't many women who see through you, Fran, but I'm one of them, so you'd better watch out,' I declared as I got to my feet.

Princess followed, though she seemed tired and was resorting to her bottom shuffle.

'What are you on about, Barby?' Fran said, looking entirely unaffected.

'Your penchant for the ladies, of course,' I giggled, teasing him back.

'The only lady I'm interested in is Betsy, so let's go and have a look at her. Come on, Princess.' Fran turned to look at the poor dog as she made her ungainly way towards the paddock. He frowned down at her, then, suddenly, an idea seemed to strike.

'Why don't you get her a prosthetic leg?' he asked.

'A what?' I replied, watching Princess helplessly, feeling something akin to a mother's anguish as she watches a beloved child struggle.

'You know, a prosthetic? A fake leg. They do them for horses, and I've seen dogs with them too. It must be worth looking into,' Fran said, opening the gate and shutting it behind him to keep Princess out of the field.

'That's probably for your protection rather than the horse's, Princess,' I laughed, leaning against the wooden post.

I watched Fran stride across the field. He had no fear when it came to horses, however wild they were. Betsy turned to look at him, then hesitated but he kept going and before long he was stroking down her brown mane and had her back leg up balanced on his knee while he inspected the foot.

'A fake leg, now why didn't I think of that?' I thought aloud. Princess's ears pricked up as I spoke. 'That could be the answer we're looking for.'

With a renewed sense of hope, I stood up and beckoned for Princess to follow.

'Let's go and see those piglets that were born the morning you arrived here. Some local schoolchildren came in and named them so I suppose they'll be named after video games or cartoon characters and I won't have a clue who they are.'

At the sty, the mother pig Dolly was rooting around in the straw, snorting loudly, while the little pigs copied her, squealing in their funny, high-pitched voices.

'Now, aren't they cute,' I said to Princess, who had flopped down onto the floor, panting with tiredness.

'You've limped a long way today, poor girl. We'll take another rest here then head back. It isn't far.' I smiled down at the dog, with real affection. Princess looked up at me, her eyes rather forlorn, and I couldn't resist the urge to kneel down next to her and stroke her beautiful face.

'I'm sorry for everything that has happened to you, Princess. Oh, I know none of it was my fault, but I'm sorry you have been so hurt . . .' her sad little face tugged at my heartstrings. I knew I already cared for her far too much, and would hate to see her go to a new home, if that were even possible.

I sighed. 'Come on, girl. Let's head back. We can go slowly, I'll follow you,' I said, watching as Princess hobbled, limped and shuffled her slow way back home.

Back at the bungalow, I called a meeting with Dan and Fran for later that day. Both men slouched in, neither removing their soil-caked wellies, and sat down heavily on the sofa.

'It's about Princess . . .' I began, but I couldn't get any further before Fran interrupted.

'She needs a prosthetic leg. I've got a friend who is a vet so I'll call her and see if we can find someone who can help,' he said, grinning at me cheekily.

'Anything else on the meeting agenda, Barby?' Dan asked, a smile playing on his lips.

'Er, no. You cheeky gits. That's it. Go and find our lovely girl a new leg, you useless men,' I retorted, making both of them burst out laughing.

At that moment Diane poked her head round the lounge door.

'What's the joke?' she said, looking between the two men.

'Nothing, nothing at all. Ask Barby . . .' chortled Dan as the pair got back up and went out to the kitchen. Seconds later the smell of toasting bread wafted out.

'They never stop eating!' I declared. Diane shrugged her shoulders, clearly unwilling to pursue the joke any further.

I sat in my chair, Princess beside me on the floor, and for the first time since Princess arrived, I felt a glimmer of hope for her and her future.

TWELVE

Disaster Strikes

'Where's Sonic today?' I looked around the kennels and was surprised when I couldn't see the funny little hound anywhere. Perhaps one of the volunteers had taken him out for an early morning walk? It wasn't like Sonic Gob to want to go out without Princess, who was still curled up in her kennel.

A young woman named Maria, who had been a volunteer at the kennels for a couple of years, came over to me. Her face looked confused and she would not catch my eye.

'Where's Sonic, Maria? Has he gone out with Fran?' I asked, again.

'No . . .' stuttered Maria. She looked extremely upset, so much so that my tone softened.

'Sorry, dear, but where is the daft chihuahua? Princess won't come out without him.'

We both looked over at Princess, who was pacing her area in her awkward way, shuffling along as she kept sniffing the edge of the wire where she and Sonic would try and snuggle up at the end of each day.

'Didn't you know?' she asked. Was I going mad, or did Maria have a look of pity on her face as she spoke?

'Know what, dear?' I was starting to feel my temper rise. What on earth was going on?

'Oh, Barby, I can't believe no-one told you . . .'

'Told me what?'

I tried to keep my temper under control. What was wrong with everyone today?

'He's been rehomed.'

The silence that followed was filled with shock.

'He's been what, dear?' I was sure I hadn't heard her properly. Everyone knew that Princess and Sonic were best friends and came as a twosome. None of my team would ever have dreamed of parting them.

'He can't have been rehomed. I would never allow it. What's happened to Sonic Gob?' My voice had risen a pitch, making the young woman tremble.

'Barby, listen, someone came in yesterday. She had already been checked out for a dog that didn't end up going with her a couple of months ago, so when she said she wanted Sonic, we thought it was fine to let her take him . . .' Poor girl. She must've been shaking on the spot as she told me the awful truth.

'You rehomed Sonic Gob?'

There was that silence again, this time filled with my

rage and utter disbelief. I felt a surge of anger, and something else, an urge to weep uncontrollably. I tried to stay calm as a rush of emotions grappled for dominance.

'Princess will never cope without him. This should never have happened. Blast it, who the hell was in charge?' I eventually spluttered.

How could anyone have been so thoughtless, so uncaring towards the boxer, to rehome her best friend, the dog that had helped her to become mobile, the hound that followed her night and day as her protector. This was one blow too many. Somehow, the shock of the past few months, with my father's sudden illness, and the looming court battle, had brought me to this: a place of total despair.

Tears pricked my eyes but my pride was still intact so I refused to cry in front of this girl, who, to her credit, looked as upset as I felt as she witnessed my distress.

'All of my team knew that I wanted Sonic and Princess to stay together.' Even as I said it, though, I knew with a sinking feeling that I had never explicitly informed the volunteers that Sonic shouldn't be rehomed.

'I was in charge, Barby. I'm really sorry; I had no idea Sonic was off-limits with finding a new owner. It was me who sorted the paperwork and documentation, I'm so sorry . . .'

Maria's voice trailed off. She looked down at her Converse trainers, biting her lip, looking devastated. She had jet-black hair and tattoos up her arms and was another gentle soul.

I'd liked her immensely when I first shared a tea break with her. She was a quiet person, unassuming, and she'd had a troubled background. The sanctuary had become a replacement for her home life; something I saw in many of the people who worked here. So many came from broken homes or from controlling or abusive parents or relationships, and, somehow, looking after animals was healing for them. The animals were dependent upon them, and this allowed their natural tenderness as human beings to resurface.

I couldn't shout at her, she looked too upset. It was a mistake in my eyes, an enormous one both for Sonic and for Princess, but deep down, I knew she would never have done it out of malice.

'There's nothing we can do about it. We can't ring the woman and say we need Sonic back. Don't worry, I'll just have to live with it, goodness knows how, and hope that Princess is able to forget her friend . . .'

Again, we both looked to Princess. She had her head down on her big paw and was whimpering softly. She looked up at us, her eyes like liquid sadness, and I felt my heart break anew.

'It's a disaster for her. I don't know how this will affect her progress. I have a feeling it will be a giant setback for her,' I said, tears welling up in my eyes.

'I'll take her with me today. Pass me Sonic's blankets. At least she didn't take all of his bedding. Perhaps Princess will be comforted by the smell of her friend.'

Maria handed me the blanket without a word.

'I'm so sorry, Barby,' she said again, her voice trembling.

'Don't worry, dear, we'll just have to cope,' I replied, my voice kind.

I carried Princess over to the bungalow, setting her down onto Sonic's blanket, which she sniffed and sniffed before curling into a tight ball and staring over at me, her eyes full of reproach.

Throughout the day, Princess periodically shuffled around the house, catching the traces of Sonic Gob's scent before admitting defeat and lying back down again, her eyes filled with confusion and pain. As I watched her, I felt the agony the dear dog must've been feeling. Her best friend in the world had gone. Princess did not understand, and her confusion, and the loss, affected us both greatly.

Helped by the chihuahua, Princess's character had come more to the fore. She had become playful, delighting in her friend's company and the games they managed to play despite the pup's disability. Princess was also a very gentle dog, who rolled with Sonic but never tried to bite him or bark defensively. She seemed to take Sonic's continual noise and games in good spirit. It was so like a boxer to behave that way. The breed is known for their love of company and their fierce loyalty. They are intelligent dogs and love to play as their energy levels are usually high. They hate being left alone, and can be quite destructive if they are.

I watched Princess as she mourned the sudden disappearance of her friend, unable to work because I couldn't shake how angry I felt at Sonic being given away.

Just then, Fran stuck his head round the door.

'I didn't hear you come in, dear,' I said, hardly looking over at him, so absorbed was I with Princess's unhappiness.

'I came in through the back. What's the matter, Barby?' had quickly learnt that Fran was very observant, and was usually the first to pick up when something was wrong.

I sighed a long, heavy sigh.

'That doesn't sound good,' Fran said, slumping down onto the leather armchair nearest to me.

'It's Sonic Gob. You won't believe it, but they rehomed him without telling me. Princess is bereft and I feel the same. Honestly, sometimes I don't know why I keep going with the place. I've had enough, Fran.'

Fran was wise enough to let my words sink into the space. After a long pause, he spoke.

'It's the kindest thing to do, Barby.'

Well, I hadn't expected him to say that. I glared at him.

'What are you on about?' I asked gruffly.

'Honestly, Barby, it's the kindest thing. Look, when Princess is rehomed, she wouldn't have been able to take Sonic with her,' Fran said gently.

'Why wouldn't she?' I asked, rather churlishly. I was pouting, much like I had as a child, though deep down, I knew Fran was right.

'Because Princess comes with her own issues, and it would be highly unlikely that someone would take two dogs if one was disabled and needed extra care. You know that's the truth.'

I shrugged, still unwilling to admit that Fran was right.

'But I've got some good news.' Fran smiled. 'Let me make you some tea and I'll tell you about it.'

'It'd better be good news or I'll have your guts for garters,' I said pompously, then, turning to the stricken dog, the tone of my voice softened as I said, 'Darling, let's hope Fran has found a new leg for you. You deserve a chance to run free again, poor creature.'

Princess barely moved. She lifted one eyebrow, then sunk back down into her grief.

'Oh, Princess, you're worse than I thought. How will you get over this, eh, girl?' I whispered, my eyes filling with tears again.

A minute later, Fran came back into the room with two cups of hot tea. He placed mine carefully on my desk then sat down.

'Right, what is it then? As I said, it'd better be good,' I huffed.

'It is, sort of. I've done the research on building a pros- thetic for Princess and at the moment it seems we'd have to go to America to get one done.'

'America!' I interrupted.

'Hold your horses, Barby, I haven't finished. Yes, America, which is obviously out of the question. But I've found a man who makes fake legs for donkeys. He's based in Dorset but is coming up this way next week, so I've asked him to come here and see if there's anything he can do for Princess.'

I nodded. 'It's a little bit of hope,' I said.

Fran nodded. 'Yes, though it might come to nothing. Obviously donkeys' legs and dogs' legs are different, but he sounds like he's got all the skills we'd need, and it won't be as punishingly expensive as flying Princess to the States.'

'No, I see that,' I mused. 'Alright, thank you, Fran. Let's hope this man will have a solution for our pup. In the meantime, I'm going to write about her in our next newsletter. It's time to find her a forever home, especially now that Sonic has gone. I just hope she recovers from this latest blow.'

'I think that's sensible, Barby. You've grown pretty attached to her so I know it won't be easy for you,' Fran added, sipping his drink.

I nodded.

Princess sighed from her position on Sonic's blanket. Would she ever get through this?

'So, can I take Dad home yet?' I was standing at the nurses' station, hands on hips, hoping they wouldn't be able to say no to me. They all knew me by now and so they grinned in response.

'You again,' one of them tutted, though her eyes sparkled with humour. She was a middle-aged lady with dark brown hair and a kind smile.

'Yes, me again. I won't take no for an answer this time. I appreciate all you've done for him, but Dad's getting no benefit from being here at this point. He knows enough to know he isn't at home and he needs to be where he's loved,' I said, hoping they would understand.

'Alright, Barby. I have to say, I agree with you. He'll be much happier at the sanctuary with you, but we'll need to do a house check first to make sure that where he's going will be suitable for him,' she answered. 'Let me organise that for you and I'll be back.'

'Thank you, nurse,' I said, sighing with relief before heading down to tell Dad the good news.

I was pleased to find that he was having a good day, and was sitting up in bed watching television.

'Hello, dearest.' I smiled as I pulled open his curtains. 'Let's get these open so you can have some daylight. It's a lovely warm spring day and the sun is shining.'

'Thank you, dear,' he replied, blinking as the daylight streamed in.

'You're looking so much better, that's really good. I'm glad to see that as I may have some good news for you.'

Dad turned his beloved face to me. His skin was as white as his sheets and his hands trembled as he tried to heave himself up on his pillows.

'Don't exert yourself, Dad. Here, let me,' I said, plumping them up and pulling him into a more comfortable position.

'How would you like to come home?' I said, beaming at him.

Dad's eyes moistened and even though he didn't speak, I could see how much it meant to him.

'We just have to wait for the hospital to do their home checks and we can rehome you, just like one of our dogs,' I chuckled.

Dad's face was still rather lopsided. His left side had been worse than his right, yet he managed a wonky smile. I patted his hand just as a nurse approached.

'Miss Keel?'

'Yes, that's me,' I replied.

'We can do the house check tomorrow, Wednesday, in the morning, as there's been a cancellation.'

'That's wonderful news,' I almost shouted with joy. 'Dad, did you hear that? We'll be rehoming you in no time.'

The next day, the inspectors came to the sanctuary and, after looking round Dad's annexe, showed me the report. Everything was fine except I needed to replace the rugs with one single carpet and put in a rail to lean on.

'Consider it done,' I said. 'My team will have carpet fitted by tonight, I can assure you. Can Dad come home tomorrow if we get it all done today?' I was desperate to get him home.

'I don't see why not,' the orderly replied, taking his clipboard and report back to the unit.

Within the hour the bedroom had been cleared of all furniture and rugs. I went out to the local carpet store and bought a section large enough to fit, and by teatime on that same day, the lads had laid the carpet and replaced all the furniture. Meanwhile, a couple of the lads had been out to buy the rail and had fixed it to Dad's wall. The room was ready, which meant my father could come home where he belonged.

The next day, the hospital was as good as their word. They let Fran and me come and pick him up, Fran wheeling him to the car in a wheelchair, while I carried his bag and medications.

Dad suffered the journey home with gentle grace. He sat staring out of the front passenger window while I rode behind him, trying not to cry. Dad's mobility was very poor, which is why the hospital had insisted that the rugs be removed to prevent him slipping up. His faculties were reduced. Sometimes I wasn't sure if he knew who I was or where he was. He hummed to himself, which seemed to soothe him, but I saw that my father was a very sick man and would need palliative care for the last chapter of his long life.

When we arrived home, Princess was curled up in the sitting room, but she made no attempt to shuffle over to greet us, so great was her depression at losing Sonic. Looking at them both, it dawned on me I had two souls to care for now: Dad and Princess. The only remedy I knew was to continue loving them both fiercely.

THIRTEEN

First Visit

Di and I were in the FIV area of the cattery, cleaning the litter trays of the cats infected with the feline form of the AIDS virus. There was no danger of transmitting it to us as the virus didn't cross to humans, but we always made sure we used the alcohol gel afterwards, as we did after handling any of the animals.

Di was carrying a stack of tins of cat food.

'Do you need a hand with that?' I called.

'No, Barby, I'm fine, all in a day's work,' she said over her shoulder.

Diane was unfeasibly strong. She often helped the lads when they were cementing new pathways or lugging new fence posts from the workshops to wherever they were needed. As ever, I was extremely grateful for her hard work.

I poured clean litter into each of the cat trays before emitting a huge sigh.

'Princess still on your mind?' Diane said as she opened up a tin and proceeded to fill a bowl with food.

At the sight and smell of Di's work, several of the cats appeared as if from nowhere, their tails high, ready for their breakfast. Amid the yowls from the hungry felines, Di stopped and looked at me.

'What is it?' she said, putting down the fork and batting away one of the braver moggies who had got too close to the food. 'No, that's not your bowl, Florrie, this one is yours. You're going to have to wait a moment longer, I'm afraid.'

I couldn't concentrate on the work. My thoughts were racing ahead to the court case the next day.

'It's that blinkin' Noise Abatement Order, isn't it? The appeal is tomorrow, right?' Di asked.

I could only nod my response.

'Yes, it's tomorrow. I feel sick to my stomach. If they go against our appeal, we could lose the renewal of our sanctuary planning permission even though we've fully complied with all the conditions set out in our original planning application,' I said miserably. 'If we lose, not only will we be unable to take in any more dogs, but it could threaten the existence of the sanctuary itself, and all because of neighbours who are moving away anyway.'

I must've looked very glum, because Di came over and sat down beside me on one of the plastic chairs.

'You don't know that for sure, Barby. Try not to get upset before the appeal has even begun. And besides, you're not alone with this, you know. Half the sanctuary is coming with you to support you,' Di said with a small smile.

'They are?' I asked, surprised.

'Of course! As if we'd let you go to court by yourself. We know how important this is. There are about twenty volunteers from the shelter who will accompany you, and they're all going to wear the Barby Keel Animal Sanctuary tops to show how much support you have. Of course, I'll stay here and look after your dad, but the rest will go.'

I was speechless, overcome with a mixture of pride and gratitude. Tears sprang to my eyes yet again, and I had to wipe them away, tutting at my lack of fortitude.

Eventually, I managed to stutter: 'Thank you, that's so very . . . very . . . kind of you all.'

'Of course, Barby, what do you expect from us? We know how worried you must be, and we know how important the work we do here is. Without your sanctuary, where would the FIV cats go, for a start? They'd be killed or left for dead, as there are very few places that will take them. And what would happen to the pigs abandoned in a farmer's field that we had to rescue? Or the lame horse that turned out to be too expensive to keep? They'd all be abandoned, left to die in their fields and paddocks.

'Can't you see? And besides, what you do here isn't just vital for animals, it helps so many people too. Look at the lads from the rehab centre who come here each week. Some of them have found new confidence and new strength to quit their drinking or using because of this place. And the bikers who raised money for the cattery! Who would've thought that a scary bunch of bikers would care about kittens?

'You bring out something precious in people, something worth all the trouble you encounter along the way.'

'What's that, dearest?' I asked, turning my tearful face to my old friend.

'Hope,' Di said, simply. 'You bring hope.'

Di's words echoed in my ears the next day as we made our way to Hastings Magistrates' Court for my appeal against Rother District Council. Di had been right. More than twenty of my motley crew came with us, arriving separately at the court, and all wearing the same top with our logo on it. I felt like I was going in with an army.

The neighbours who lived in the house, which sat right next to the entrance of the sanctuary, were there. They were a rather ordinary-looking couple, certainly no-one I would have thought could cause such concern and upset to us, but then people can do some strange and hurtful things – we knew that well enough.

A judge was presiding, making the whole thing rather surreal.

Rother District Council laid out its case. Apparently, the neighbours had recorded the dogs barking in the kennels, claiming they were barking for nineteen hours a day.

I couldn't help myself. I spluttered, 'Nineteen hours, that's impossible! No dog could bark for that long; they wouldn't have any throat left!'

'Shhhhh,' my barrister warned me. 'It's really important that you keep calm, Barby.'

'How can I?' I hissed.

'Barby, please be calm. It's best to appear as reasonable as possible. Please, let me handle it.'

I sat back, folding my arms, and glaring at the couple who had brought the case against me.

When it came to our turn to make our arguments for appeal, my legal man was very good. He said that as we had only seven kennels, and as dogs came in and out of the kennels over the period in question, it was impossible to have had the barking for that length of time. He also made the point that, if animal noise upset the complainants, why they would buy a house next to a sanctuary was beyond anyone's understanding.

I tittered at this, but after a sharp glance from the barrister, I stayed quiet for the rest of the case.

When at last I was given a chance to speak, I stood up, trembling a little, and spoke, as ever, from the heart. I hadn't rehearsed a speech but I knew what I wanted to say.

'My dogs do bark, but that's what dogs do, but not to the extent that has been alleged.

'The dogs that come to my sanctuary are bewildered, and some have been very badly treated, so it is no wonder that they can be distressed or upset at times. We do our best to comfort and settle them, but yes, there are a few dogs that need a bit of extra understanding, as some do bark more than others. I've lived on the land for thirty years, and run the sanctuary for more than twenty years, and in all that time, I've never received a single complaint before.

'I ask the court, what will happen to these unfortunate dogs if the abatement is upheld? Because if it is upheld, then it means only taking in dogs that do not bark, if any such dogs exist. If my neighbours can tell me how to stop a frightened or abused dog barking, then I would gladly listen to them.'

I looked directly at the couple as I said this, and was gratified to see them both looking uncomfortable.

I continued: 'At the end of the day, they knew the sanctuary was there when they bought their house. We've had hundreds of letters of support from the rest of our neighbours, and those who have helped or needed us. We've included some of them in our court documents, Your Honour.'

With that, I sat down after bowing to the judge.

The judge smiled at me and my heart skipped a beat. He looked sympathetic. Could this mean we could actually win this appeal? Once he'd read the letters, all of which praised our work and dismissed the allegations made by the couple, he couldn't possibly not let us win, could he?

When the judge asked for time to deliberate, I shot a triumphant smile to my barrister. I was convinced the judge was on our side.

We waited outside the court room in a larger area with metal chairs bolted to the floors, sipping weak tea from the small café that operated in the main waiting area. We were a crowd, and I was buoyed up, thinking of the judge's warm smile and how he'd appeared to listen to every word we said.

'Don't count your chickens, Barby. You don't know what the judge was thinking. They're very experienced at listening to both sides of an argument though, and whatever the result is, you will have to accept it,' the barrister said.

I turned to look at the couple who were sitting as far away from us as they could.

Ten minutes later, we were called back into the wooden-walled court room. The couple were sitting to our left, with their barrister and mine sitting between us.

We rose as the judge walked in. His face had changed. He looked stern, and my heart skipped a beat again, but this time, I felt sick as we waited for him to deliver his verdict.

He upheld the Noise Abatement Order and dismissed our appeal. I felt like I'd been given a slap around the face.

'But you can't . . .' I said, looking round the room wildly as if for someone or something to help us, but there was no one there, nothing to stop the terrible truth. We'd lost our case. Was this the end of the sanctuary?

My heart pounding, tears threatening to come yet again, I felt shock waves overwhelm me. I knew this would affect how many dogs we could look after at any one time, and the thought of having to turn away an animal in need was too much to bear.

After the judge had read out his verdict, he asked the council what they wanted us to pay towards their court costs. I hadn't realised, but the loser had to pay towards the cost of bringing the case against them. The unfairness of it all stung.

'Two thousand pounds, please, Your Honour,' was the reply.

I gasped. 'We can't afford that,' I cried. I didn't care how rude I sounded by this stage. I couldn't believe we had lost our appeal. I was gutted, and I knew all my supporters in the lobby would be devastated too.

The judge turned to me and asked: 'How much can you afford? Would five hundred pounds be manageable?'

It was an act of kindness, and so I nodded gratefully.

A generous supporter offered to pay the fine for us, which was another blessing. My motley crew were furious, but I'd had enough. As I walked down the steps of the magistrates' court towards Fran's parked car, all I could think about was Princess. She was my priority now, not the council, not the sound of barking dogs or the worry that the shelter might shut. Suddenly, none of that seemed important any more.

'You look like you've had an epiphany, Barby,' said Fran as he drove us home.

'D'you know what, I think I have. Today I realised that the only thing that's important is the vulnerable creatures in our care, and for me, that means Princess. She needs a forever home and I'm going to do everything in my power to find her one,' I said, smiling over at Fran. 'And if the council ever tries to take away my planning permission, they'll have an almighty fight on their hands.'

'That's the spirit,' he replied, turning into our driveway, his tyres making a crunching sound on the gravel.

Outside, the sign that announced our sanctuary had recently been given a fresh coat of paint as part of the renovations before our spring reopening. The hedges had been cut back, and there were wild primroses peeking out from the floor of the kennel run that lay to the right.

As we arrived, the dogs started up a chorus, barking to welcome us home.

'That should annoy them, at least.' I grinned to Fran, who started to laugh.

'Still the same old hag! At least losing the appeal didn't change you, Barby, thank goodness.'

Back inside, I got out my phone book and started to ring round, putting the word out that we had an adorable year-old boxer dog who needed extra love and care. Dan had taken a photo of Princess and included it in our latest newsletter, calling out for new owners, and describing what a lovely dog she was growing into.

'There she is, she looks very handsome, though you can't really see that her leg is missing from the angle,' Di said, squinting at the newly printed newsletter.

'I know, I saw that too. I don't know if Dan intended to hide it or whether Princess just wouldn't play ball and pose properly. Either way, she's a very beautiful girl . . .'

We both stood for a moment, reflecting on the dog and her future, which somehow, in that moment, seemed less uncertain.

By Sunday, I had a couple who were interested in rehoming a boxer puppy. I don't know why, but I hadn't mentioned the fact she had a leg missing. I knew it was wrong, but deep down I hoped they would see through her disability and love her for the gorgeous soul she was.

The couple who were coming had rung in to the sanctuary purely by chance, asking to visit the dogs. I'd explained to them that we had five Staffies and a boxer puppy, and I could tell by the tone of their voice that they preferred the sound of Princess.

'We look forward to seeing you,' I'd said, punching the air as I put the phone down, much to Diane's delight.

'I know I'll be devastated to see her go but I know this is the right thing to do. She needs all the love and attention she can get, and even though I try my hardest to spend time with Princess, I have so much work to do I just can't give her what she needs,' I said to my friend.

Diane nodded her approval: 'I think you're right. She needs a loving new home, and if anyone can find her one, it's you, Barby.'

I was full of hope for Princess. We were now in my favourite month, May, early summertime, and the couple arrived just before the open afternoon we held every Sunday. I was eagerly waiting at the gate to meet them.

They were younger than I'd expected them to be, in their early forties, a childless couple looking for a dog after their former rescue dog had died a year earlier.

'We're only just ready to let another dog into our life,' the woman, a smart-looking lady called Margaret, explained. Her husband, James, held back, his hands in his pockets, and seemed to be a rather shy person from what I could see.

Margaret did all the talking. She chatted away as we walked the few paces to the kennels, telling me about her first dog, a greyhound. They wanted another high-energy hound because they both liked to hike.

'As I said on the telephone, we have five Staffordshire bull terriers, all of whom are lovely dogs, though they tend to bark a bit. Staffies are always harder to rehome because they have a bad reputation, though I've never fathomed out why. If they misbehave or become aggressive, it's usually because they've been treated badly or trained to be like that. A well-trained, well-cared-for Staffie is a delight to foster.

'Princess is the boxer. She's just over a year old . . .' My voice trailed off. We'd reached the door to the kennels.

How can they not fall for her? I thought to myself as we walked to Princess's pen. *Those big brown, melting eyes and that sweet square face are enough to make anyone fall in love with her.*

As we reached the pen, Princess was sitting down. When she saw me, her tail started to wag.

'Boxers usually have their tails docked but she hasn't. Again, we don't know why.'

'She's gorgeous,' said the woman, kneeling down a few paces away from her.

'We do ask people not to approach the dogs but to let them approach you. They need to sniff you out first, make sure they feel safe.' I was gabbling a bit because I so desperately wanted them to love her the way I did, to see past her missing limb.

At that precise moment, Princess staggered to her three feet, wobbling as she moved and revealing her missing limb. There was a stunned silence.

Princess moved again, ungainly as she turned, then, using her front paw to propel her forward, she pushed herself along on her bottom.

Margaret stood up abruptly. 'Oh dear, poor thing,' was all she said. She didn't need to say more. I heard the rejection, the disappointment in her voice.

'She's such a lovely dog,' I said 'We really don't want her to go. We've been looking into a prosthetic leg for her to help her have a normal life.'

'I don't think . . . would you mind if we looked at the others? She's a very pretty dog but we're looking for a pet that can walk with us. I'm sorry, but I don't think it will work.'

Margaret looked to her husband, who just nodded.

I bit my tongue, feeling so stupid for not warning them, and so bad for Princess that she had encountered another rejection.

'Of course, you can see the others. See you later, Princess,' I said, leaning down to stroke her folded ears.

I watched as Margaret petted and stroked the others, picking out one of the Staffies, a three-year-old dog called Maud, to go for a walk around the site.

When they returned, an hour later, Margaret gave me the nod. 'We'd like to take this one. She's adorable, and she loves walking.'

'Alright, dear. I'll take you to the house and we can complete the necessary checks. We'll need to do a home check at your place before we can let Maud go, and you'll need to fill out some forms.'

I looked back at Princess. She was sitting by her doorway, staring after the couple as they left. She gave a small wag of her tail and her head sunk onto her paw, giving a long, sad sigh.

FOURTEEN

Please Love Me

I'd learned my lesson from that first visit. I felt that in not telling the couple about the hound's missing limb, I'd somehow caused the rejection once they discovered it, a fact I found hard to live with afterwards.

'Why didn't I tell them before they came? That was such a stupid thing to do. Princess's face when she backed off away from her, well, she looked devastated,' I said to Diane that evening.

'You did what you thought was right, Barby. Don't give yourself a hard time. We all make mistakes, and you thought that they would fall in love with her despite, or maybe even because of, her disability.' Di's words were intended to comfort me but I knew I'd done the wrong thing in 'forgetting' to tell them that she only had three legs.

I sighed. My grumpy dog Harry harrumphed as he slumped down beside me.

'Oh, remembered me, have you?' I said, giving his long whitish-blonde fur a tickle.

'At least you've been given your planning permission so you know the court case hasn't affected the sanctuary's future,' Di reasoned, trying to cheer me up.

Obviously I'd been delighted to hear that news, but everything paled in front of the problem that was Princess, and whether she would ever find a home.

I nodded to Diane but didn't say a word.

Meanwhile, Harry had all but disowned me since Princess had come along. I'd put his nose out of joint by spending so much time and energy on the pup, and he hadn't liked it one bit.

'It isn't like you to be jealous,' I said to Harry as he submitted to my endearments with good grace.

The only response I got from him was a big yawn before casting me an accusing glance.

I laughed at that.

'Just because I love Princess, and want the best for her, doesn't mean I don't love you any more, daft mutt.' Harry had taken to sleeping in Dad's room on the floor, but perhaps that wasn't disgust at my affections being supplanted by Princess; maybe he was protecting my father, sensing, as animals do, that his end was near.

I was caring for Dad myself, and had been since he came home in the springtime. Each morning, I washed him, made him breakfast and helped him to eat it. On good days, he might get dressed and potter into the lounge and sit with me until he got tired; on bad days, he'd stay in bed, watching television, while various members of staff and friends would check in on him.

I'd installed an urn in the kitchen so that I wouldn't have to keep boiling endless kettles for his cups of tea, and somehow, we all got on with the work of the sanctuary as well. I wouldn't have had it any other way. My dad deserved to be cared for by those who loved him. He was the only man in my life who hadn't ever let me down, and I would never have forgiven myself if I'd left him to die on a hospital ward. On a sad note, two days after Dad left the ward and our visits to Bill stopped, the poor old soul died. Proof, if any were needed, that connection, be it human or animal, makes us want to live.

Unfortunately, the idea of making a false leg for Princess had been roundly squashed by the expert Fran had called upon for help.

He'd arrived on a warm day in early summer. Fran met the man, Paul, at the gate and walked over to the kennels where I was waiting with Princess.

'This could be the start of a whole new life for you,' I whispered to the dog. She was in a playful mood and I'd been throwing cuddly toys for her to shuffle after and kill with a growl and shake of her gorgeous head.

'Hello, I'm Barby Keel,' I said with a smile as the chap from the West Country entered the pen.

'Hello, and this must be Princess. Hello, girl,' the man said. He seemed very nice; his movements gentle as he crouched next to the dog.

'So, you've had a bit of an accident. Do you mind if I take a quick look?' he crooned. Princess seemed to know immediately that she was in safe hands, and she let the chap pick her up and inspect the stump, which was fully healed.

'What a beautiful dog you are! How old is she?' Paul asked, turning to me.

'She's a year old. She came to us eight months ago. She's an absolute sweetie but her injury really affects her quality of life. Boxers are so energetic and love to dash about, which is obviously very hard for her. I think she might be a bit depressed because of it. She isn't raring to go. We have to give her a lot of encouragement to play or move about, which isn't like a boxer puppy at all,' I replied, giving Princess's nut-brown fur a stroke. I was satisfied to see how sleek she was looking these days. The dandruff had cleared up as her nutrition had improved, and other than her unfortunate leg, she was in very good condition.

'Well, I think I'd be depressed if I suddenly found I couldn't move about properly. Anyone, animal or human, goes through a mourning period if they find themselves suddenly disabled, it's natural.'

'Do your donkeys experience that too?' I'd asked. I found this man fascinating. It was a pretty niche job, making prosthetics for donkeys and horses.

'Yes, some of them do. Though they are much better than us humans at getting on with it and living life,' he said. He was feeling down the small stump, which made Princess wince, but she was good as gold, and didn't move an inch.

'Okay, well, I'm sorry to say that it isn't good news.' The man put Princess down, stroking her head and ears as he did so.

I felt my stomach twist. My hopes had been pinned on this encounter, so convinced had I been that Princess's immobility could be solved. I had been so concerned with how we might go about raising the money for a fake leg for Princess that I hadn't given any thought to the possibility that it might not happen at all. I looked at Paul's face and knew what he was about to say.

He shook his head. 'I'm afraid it can't be done.' He said it matter-of-factly, though not without sympathy.

'Her stump is too short. The amputation was done far too high on her leg to allow us to make her a prosthetic. There's not enough leg to fit anything to. She'll have to stay as she is, I'm afraid.'

It was a severe blow. I'd convinced myself that once Princess had a new leg, we'd be able to find her a home right away. Seeing the prospect of that disappear so abruptly was a shock.

'There's really nothing you can do?' I asked, hearing the desperation in my voice.

He shook his head again.

We both looked down at Princess, who was gnawing on her favourite chew toy. She seemed oblivious to the bad news swirling above her head.

'You could try asking an expert in America, who specialises in dog prosthetics, but I'm afraid it's likely that they'll say the same, and it might be a costly exercise to hear the same news in the end,' he added, getting up off the floor.

'She's a lovely dog. I'm sure someone will want her as she is.'

'I hope you're right,' I sighed. 'It's been very kind of you to come and see her, anyway. I can't thank you enough,' I said sincerely, ushering him out.

Outside the kennels the air was sweet with summer. It was late afternoon and the trees were thick with birds, the air filled with their chatter. Over in the paddock a horse neighed, and there was a distant sound of the sheep baaa-ing.

'Feeding time,' I said by way of explanation.

'It's a lovely spot you have here. You should come down to the West Country and see the horse and donkey sanctuary there. We're surrounded by rolling fields too.'

I chuckled at that: 'I never get the time to leave the shelter. We're always short-staffed even though we have a team of volunteers, and we have to spend a lot of time fundraising. Perhaps one day I'll take a holiday, but it hasn't yet happened in twenty years.'

It was true. Once the animals had started to come and live on my land, I don't think I'd ever spent a night away from the place by choice. The only times I left the land was for an elective hysterectomy, which had kept me in hospital for eight nights, and the surgery I had to remove a cancerous lump in my breast. Apart from that, you couldn't drag me away. I was as much a part of the air we breathed and the soil we walked on as any creature here. To leave the site would've been torture to me. I ran the place. Without me around, who would oversee the work, cajole businesses into giving money, recruit volunteers, build new fences or make plans for the future? I had lots of help, but at the end of the day, I was responsible for every single beast, feathered or furred, sick or well, homed or resident here. They were all my responsibility, and I took that role very seriously.

The man smiled as if he knew exactly what I was thinking.

'Well, I'll be off then. Good luck with Princess.'

I waved him off.

'She's going to need it,' I muttered under my breath before walking back to the kennels.

Autumn was now approaching. Princess had been available for rehoming since May, and had been with us at the sanctuary for a little over a year now. Yet, despite a stream of visitors looking to adopt a dog, no one ever seemed to be able, or willing, to take her on. I couldn't count how many times the dear pup had tried to race towards a person, only to be greeted by a frozen smile, or a step back in momentary shock as the sight of her mangled leg greeted them.

Every time, *every single time*, the people made their excuses and left. Princess's subsequent dismay and my heartbreak at the continual rejection were proving too much for me to bear. The older she got, the less likely it was that someone would take a shine to a disabled dog. A beautiful puppy with three legs was one thing, but a fully grown dog was quite another, sad though it was to admit.

I put up posters of her with a picture and an explanation about her leg. I rang prospective foster families, telling them straight away that she had a disability. People came to see her. Each weekend there was someone new, but as soon as they saw how badly affected Princess was by the missing limb, their interest waned. It was heartbreaking to watch the same thing happening again and again, as it did today.

Princess stared up at the man, her eyes pools of love, her tongue hanging out, panting slightly.

I caught my breath, hoping and praying that this time, *this time*, it would work out for the beleaguered dog. I exchanged glances with Fran, knowing he was just as keen as I was to get Princess settled, and just as nervous at this latest in a long line of introductions.

'Do you think he likes her?' I hissed to Fran.

'Shhh, Barby, wait and see. He's going into the pen so it's looking fairly good,' Fran replied. We were standing behind the man, a professional in his mid-forties who was recently divorced and looking for a dog for company.

'He's stroking her,' I said with glee when I saw Princess's reaction. She immediately sniffed the man's hand then gave it a lick.

Then it all went horribly wrong.

Princess tried to get up but her tail was wagging so fiercely that it toppled her over, flat on her face again. Scrabbling to get up, Princess whined and the harder she fought to pull herself back up, the more ungainly she looked.

We watched as the inevitable happened.

Standing up and backing out of the pen, the man turned to speak to us.

He was shaking his head. 'I'm sorry. I just don't think it's going to work. She's more disabled than I thought. I just won't be able to give her enough support. Again, I'm really sorry.'

At least the man had the decency to look sorry for Princess. Many people reacted with disgust or fear, a sight that always left my heart ripped to bits for the beautiful dog on the receiving end of this treatment.

I doubted anyone was being intentionally cruel, but people came to us with a fantasy of a perfect rescue dog in their minds, and Princess just didn't fit the bill.

'Never mind. It's best you work that out now. We wouldn't want to rehome Princess and find it wasn't going to work for her. Thank you, shall I see you out?' I said in a monotone voice. I couldn't recall how many times I'd said something similar over the past few months.

'Thank you, and sorry again. I can see she's a lovely dog.'

'She is,' I answered stoutly in Princess's defence. I was so protective of my animals. I couldn't bear to see the dog rejected over and over again.

After the gentleman had left, I returned to Princess's pen and sat with her. Her eagerness at being stroked, at being given whatever affection she could glean from me, made me want to cry.

Princess rolled onto her back, exposing her tummy and throwing her three remaining limbs in the air. The stump was fully healed but would never make a pretty sight, yet I could only feel intense love for her. That day I stayed sitting with the dog for a long time after everyone had left.

Even though by all accounts we'd just had a successful day at the sanctuary – the tea rooms had sold out of cakes as demand was so high, two of the Staffies were now going to good homes, and three cats had been chosen to be fostered – the pain of having my hopes rise every time someone expressed an interest in a disabled dog, only to have them dashed, was becoming too much.

FIFTEEN

Hopes Dashed

The hours passed slowly as I sat by my father's bedside and read to him, or told him the latest news of the sanctuary. Dad was almost entirely bedridden now, and the once-proud, independent animal lover was reduced to a frail little old man, unable to care for any of the beasts on the site, unable to do anything at all. Now it was my turn to help him, and I did so gladly.

Each morning, I woke at first light to the sound of the birds singing the dawn chorus in the ash trees that stood at the boundary of the land. This would, in turn, set off the cockerels, chickens, geese and peacocks, which would crow and cackle, screech and scratch as they welcomed the new day in glorious liberated sound.

I would yawn and stretch, making Harry do the same. The great spaniel would stand up from his bed on the rug on the floor, and sit there, staring at me in his bossy way until I gave in and got out of bed.

'Alright, alright, Harry. You really are such a naughty brute. Why can't you be a bit more cheerful in the mornings, or at any time, really?' I would laugh. The sight of his long nose, his indignant-looking expression, never failed to amuse me. He really was the grumpiest dog I'd ever come across.

'Come on, let's go and get you some food. What a pickle you are.' I would stroke him, if he let me, then pull on my work clothes for the day. I always wore the same thing: a Barby Keel Animal Sanctuary fleece top and a pair of comfortable old trousers tucked into boots. In winter I added a warm gilet and a scarf, in summer I'd wear a T-shirt emblazoned with the same motif.

I had never cared about clothes. For me, they were a means to cover myself and be as comfortable as possible while I did physical work. I'd been wearing the same combination for more years than I could remember.

Now that I was looking after Dad, there didn't seem any point changing my outfit, or routine. After feeding Harry, I'd pour Dad a mug of milky tea and make him a couple of slices of toast with butter and his favourite marmalade. I'd knock before entering his annexe, saying brightly: 'Good morning, Dad. How did you sleep? Did you have a good night?'

These days he would always still be lying there rather than trying to get up or sitting up against his pillows.

My father wouldn't answer. Instead, he'd blink at the sound of my voice and try to raise his head.

'Don't exert yourself, Dad. Let me help you,' I'd say, putting down the tray with his breakfast on and rushing to his bedside. The sight of him unable to lift himself up when he'd been such a strong, outdoors type, was on some days more than I could bear.

His skin was pale to the point of being translucent, his hair was just thin wisps of white now. He couldn't hold up a spoon to feed himself, or even the toast I had ready for him. I would patiently sit by him, holding the toast to his lips while he chewed on minuscule pieces. These days, it could take him more than half an hour just to eat a slice of toast.

I'd seen him go from gardening and feeding animals to this in less than a year. It was a truly devastating sight.

Luckily, my general lack of patience when it came to humans didn't extend to my father. I loved him with a passion born of an unhappy childhood, and many times I thought of how my mother seemed to know how strong our bond was, and was equally determined to break it. I have often wondered if my mum was jealous of the closeness between Dad and I. Certainly, when Dad finally left her and moved in with me, she seemed to lose much of her fierce energy, and lived rather a small, lonely life after that.

She still treated me appallingly, even though over the years I had made many attempts to reconcile. One time, a cousin had flown in from Canada and Mum had demanded my presence at an afternoon tea she'd planned to welcome the family guest. At the very last minute, we had a crisis at the sanctuary and I was unable to attend. Most people would understand that life sometimes gets in the way, and plans can change. Not my mother. When I rang to apologise, her reply was callous in the extreme: 'I don't have a daughter any longer,' and she slammed the phone down, leaving me holding the receiver in my hand, confusion and shock hitting me in equal measure.

Dad got the same treatment from her, and so the pact was made. It was me and Dad, and her and Peter, with my sister Pam in contact with both sides. Peter felt desperately sorry that Mother and I couldn't see eye to eye, and he and I always maintained our close bond through the years, until he passed away from leukaemia almost ten years ago.

Peter's death was the closest I'd ever seen my dad come to expressing emotion. He had spent a lifetime suppressing his desires, his hopes and dreams, trying unsuccessfully to please my mother, yet Peter's death almost broke him. At the time, Dad couldn't face coming to the hospital, not out of concern for himself but for Peter. Dad knew that he would be inconsolable at the sight of his bonny beloved boy laid up in a hospital bed as death approached him, stealing the golden-haired, smiling man from us forever. He couldn't go to Peter's funeral either and I knew that Dad, with his deeply kind heart and his quiet ways, would have been broken by the experience, so I never tried to talk him into going.

After Peter's death, my own grief was so all-encompassing, so filled with fury at a universe that could spare me, his younger sister, while he, the sunny, happy-go-lucky one, was taken. For weeks, I could barely see past my own grief, and it was only with the love of my dog Teddy, who always instinctively knew how I was feeling, and the support of my motley crew, that I got through it. Dad retreated into his shell, almost becoming a hermit in those days. I respected his need for privacy to come to terms with his emotions, but I also knew I couldn't leave him stranded inside his loss. It took many weeks for me to coax him back out to do his normal chores: the gardening, feeding the cats and rabbits and helping out with jobs around the site.

I persevered, and a year after Peter's death, Dad was back, pottering around the land, with all of us keeping a close eye on him as he suffered what no parent should ever have to face: the death of their child before them.

Dad didn't ever recover from the loss of Peter, I don't think. He just wasn't ever the same after that. His little jokes and games continued, but he seemed to have no heart for them, or for much else. His zest for life seemed to fade. Sadly, it wasn't the first child my father, or my mother, had grieved. Peter wasn't the first born. Their first child, a boy, had been stillborn. They didn't even name him, but I could only imagine the grief they must both have suffered. Perhaps Peter's death triggered memories of that terrible tragedy. Or perhaps, losing two children was just too much for any person to deal with.

Now, following his stroke, he was a shadow of the man he'd been. All life seemed to have leaked from him, leaving behind a confused, dependent man, who hated being alone, and would cry out in the night for me.

I'd always rush in, calm his night terrors, never sure whether he could hear me or understand what I was saying, and many times, I wept late into the night after such an episode.

Often he'd try to speak, but the sounds he made were unintelligible, though he still had a few moments of lucidity, which always filled me with a surge of hope. Even though I knew there was no coming back from his stroke, whenever he said a full sentence or looked at me with his twinkling blue eyes and appeared to understand every word, I felt that most cruel of emotions – hope – again.

I call it cruel, because the truth was, I knew deep down he would never leave his bed. There was no hope, just as I was starting to see there was no hope for Princess. No one wanted her. She looked like she was destined to stay in our kennels for the rest of her days.

Another visit had gone horribly wrong, despite all the signs initially looking good. A middle-aged couple had called in to say they wanted a rescue dog, and I told them about the Staffies we had. There were four of them at the time, and I barely mentioned Princess, believing it was virtually pointless to even talk about him.

'You have a boxer?' the woman called Joy had asked.

'Yes, but you won't want her, dear, she's only got three legs. Taking her on would be a real task. You'd have to modify your lifestyle as she can't limp very far or fast. We tried to find someone who could make her a prosthetic but it's proved impossible.'

I was actually trying to put them off. I really hated visiting days now because I couldn't bear seeing yet another rejection of the lovely dog. I felt Princess's plight keenly, and I failed to understand why people couldn't overlook her disability.

'Well, can we see her? We've always wanted a boxer and we don't mind if she limps, really we don't.' The woman sounded sincere, and reluctantly I agreed to let them come and see him.

'Okay, dear, but I'm warning you, it'd be better if you looked at the Staffies. They're all lovable dogs . . .'

'No, thank you, we'd like to see the boxer, if that's okay.'

The woman, Joy, seemed to have set her sights on her, and I felt my heart lift slightly at the thought that Princess might find her forever home after all.

I put the phone down and turned to Diane, who was sitting next to me as we took our morning break together.

Her eyebrows were arched as she'd gleaned the content of the conversation.

I couldn't help it. I smiled and my heart leapt.

'I think we might have found a home,' I said breathlessly, beaming at her.

Diane saw the excitement in my eyes, and instantly threw a necessary dampener on my new-found hopes.

'You know how it goes, Barby. You've done this enough times. Don't get your hopes up before Princess is settled with her forever family. People say things and they do genuinely want to love the animal but it's a special kind of chemistry when a new owner meets a dog. They might say they want a disabled dog but the reality is, often, a different thing.'

I scowled at Diane, even though I knew she was talking absolute sense. I so desperately wanted to believe that this time, the gorgeous girl, who let me tickle under her square chin and whisper endearments into her funny folded ears, would finally find a home.

'They are keen, believe me. This could be it,' I said, refusing to let her diminish my enthusiasm.

Di tutted and sipped her tea.

'Don't count your chickens, Barby. Look, I hate seeing you so upset when things don't work out. You can't expect other mere mortals to feel as intensely about Princess as you do, or any other dog. You've got a special bond with her, which took time, and it'll be the same for them. I don't need to tell you any of this. You've been fostering dogs for twenty-odd years and yet, you never change. Let's just see what happens.'

I snorted, calling her a pessimist, to which she'd retorted 'Realist!' and we carried on with our companionable tea break in silence.

Later that week, the couple turned up at the agreed time. 'Another good sign, they're eager beavers.' I grinned at Diane, who was with me to meet them. She shook her head in response: 'Barby . . .' she muttered as a warning.

But I wouldn't listen to reason. I was sure this couple would be the ones. Why else would they get so excited about the mention of a boxer and demand to meet her?

They had a large car, which was another good sign. 'Plenty of room for Princess . . .' I exclaimed, which made Diane sigh.

I marched over to meet them with a beaming smile on my face.

'Welcome to the sanctuary. I'm Barby and this is Diane.'

'Hello, very pleased to meet you. I'm Joy and this is Richard.' The couple looked older than I'd imagined them, and Richard looked rather frail. He had a walking stick but could walk on the gravel easily.

'Come this way,' I said, opening the gate and showing them into the yard.

At the sight of the new car, several of the dogs had started barking but I couldn't make out Princess's voice. She rarely barked, and if she did, it was normally more for fun. Boxers are good guard dogs because of their propensity to only bark if there's real need for it, such as danger approaching or the presence of a threatening stranger.

We opened the door, and the sound of excited, hopeful hounds greeted us.

'Stop making that racket,' I said as we passed down the pens.

'Are you sure you don't want to see some of the other dogs before we see Princess?' I said, but both Joy and Richard shook their heads firmly.

I noticed that Richard stumbled a little on the concrete flooring which wasn't completely flat. He smiled over at me as he noticed me watching him.

'Don't worry, I'm fine, let's see this boxer.'

Princess was sitting at the far end of his pen, chewing her favourite toy when I approached.

As soon as she knew it was me, she yelped, dropped her toy and pushed up onto her front leg.

Go on, Princess, get up and show them you can balance and limp over. I was willing this plucky dog to walk properly, as best she could.

'Come on, Princess, let's see if you can walk for us today. Walk,' I said as a command.

She ignored me. Her excitement was so acute, her tail wagged in circles, or so it appeared, her tongue lolled out of her mouth, causing a great stream of dribble to hang down, and she shifted himself towards us, dragging both legs on her bottom.

Oh Princess, why can't you just try, I thought to myself, to my shame.

I looked over at the couple and I saw the shock on their faces. They glanced at each other, and it was plain to see that their minds were already made up.

'She's a very affectionate, playful thing. In fact, she can be very boisterous with the right play and especially if there are other dogs she can play with . . .' I could hear my voice a pitch higher than usual. I knew I sounded desperate but when I saw their reaction, my stomach had hit my boots.

'Er . . . so sorry . . . she's a lovely-looking dog, but . . .' Richard started to speak.

'But she's very disabled,' Joy continued. 'We had no idea she was unable to move at all. We thought she might be able to limp around. As you can see, my husband couldn't cope with a dog that wants strenuous exercise, which is why we thought this could be the right dog.'

Neither of them met my eye.

In that moment, all the hopes I'd ever had for Princess crashed to the floor. They vanished. I knew then that she was a dog without hope, who would, most likely, live out her days with us. I loved her dearly and would be pleased to care for her, but I knew that she would be happier being part of a new family who could give her the company and adoration a boxer needs.

'I did tell you very clearly that she had three legs. I didn't mislead you in any way, but you were insistent that you still wanted to see her,' I replied, my voice steely.

'I think what Barby means is that we understand that a dog in Princess's position needs a lot of support, and has much higher needs than an abled-bodied animal,' Di interrupted, elbowing me to stop talking.

She knew I was devastated, and could fire off at any moment.

'Yes, that's what I meant,' I said dully. My heart was in bits. How could anyone not want to keep Princess? Her eyes were deep brown, her coat glossy and rich, her personality adorable. All these things were, to me, far more important than a missing leg.

'Thank you for coming, anyway,' I added, trying to put aside my hurt. 'Diane will see you out, unless you want to look at the Staffies we have . . .'

With that, I looked over at Di who gave me a small nod back, and left the kennels. I could've wept. Diane was right, as usual. I had got my hopes up. I had thought it was a done deal. How wrong could I have been? How stupid of me to expect people to see past Princess's injury.

I made a decision. I would stop advertising Princess. I would stop telling people about her. She would be one of our resident animals from this day forward, and I would never, ever, raise my hopes for her future again.

SIXTEEN

The End Approaches

I watched as Dad drew in quiet breaths, then expelled them with as little effort; small movements that pushed his pyjama-clad chest up by the merest sliver of activity, then dropped it back down, barely moving at all. His face looked peaceful, serene almost, which made me happy.

Dad slept more and more these days, leaving me with time on my hands. I knew I should be helping to prepare for the Christmas Bazaar, which by now was only a few weeks away, but I'd delegated much of the work to the charity trustees and so I felt I could take a small liberty and please myself today.

I yawned. Looking after Dad was tiring, and not just because I was often walking from various parts of the site to his bedside, checking in on him throughout each day; it was also taking a huge toll on my emotions. I knew all my care for him was leading only one way, to his eventual passing. Knowing this, yet still having to feed him, wash him, chatter to him in an upbeat way, change his bedding, help him to use the toilet, was tough on me, though I would never have let anyone else look after him.

I'd always been fiercely protective of my father, even as a child. I sensed he was a fragile soul, and often I stood between him and Mum as she let rip at him for whichever new animal was taking up precious space in our tiny home. It wasn't my place to defend him – I was only a child! Yet I couldn't bear to see him cowering beneath my mother's wrath. I always had a thicker skin than Dad. Sometimes, I thought he hadn't been made for this world with its miseries, suffering and burdens.

I shook my head to clear those thoughts and memories. It was all best left to the past. I had little time left with Dad, and I wanted to cherish each moment we had left.

'I know exactly what to do. Harry, come with me. Let's go and get Princess and go for a walk.' I whistled to my moody spaniel, who, to his credit, followed after me.

Opening the door, the cold, crisp air of the November morning hit me hard in the face. Harry took one look outside, at the pile of wind-whipped brown leaves moldering near the greenhouse, sniffed at the smoky winter scent of the freezing air, then backed off, turning his large body round in the small corridor with some difficulty, then walking off to the lounge where the fire was permanently lit.

'Harry, you're a coward,' I laughed. 'Just Princess and me, then,' I said to myself as I wrapped my scarf tighter around me and stepped out.

Fran had chosen that moment to arrive at the gate leading to my bungalow, which was fenced with chicken wire to stop the melee of geese, chickens, hens and cockerels from gaining access to my garden.

'Hello old bag, I've been looking for you,' he quipped, opening the gate and marching in.

'Well, now you've found me, but I warn you, I'm off for a walk with Princess,' I said in rather a grump. Harry would've been proud of me.

'I can see that, but I need to ask you something,' he said, grinning.

'I haven't got time, Fran. Ask someone else. Dad has just fallen asleep so I reckon I've got an hour at most to do my own thing. Honestly, can't any of you make a decision by yourselves?' I added, rather ungraciously.

'We're very happy to make decisions, but if you don't like them, you tell us off!' Fran retorted. 'It's not urgent, though, so I'll ask you later. I'll also check in on your dad in half an hour and buzz you if he wakes up.' Fran winked at me.

'Thank you, dearest, that's very kind of you. This old bag is very grateful,' I said. 'Now, please, can I go for my walk?'

Fran stepped aside, performing a flourishing bow as I passed.

'And enough of your cheek,' I laughed. 'You'll be the death of me, Fran. Go and get some work done.'

'Yes, madam, and don't forget that I need to speak to you.'

By the time I'd reached the kennels, a low building with a shiny new roof and the seven pens that contained four remaining dogs, including my three-legged friend, I'd already forgotten the business of the day. Whenever I spent time with Princess, my worries always seemed to recede at the sight of her joyful greeting, in spite of her impeded mobility. I would gain perspective over my life. Things weren't really that bad: Dad was well cared for, safe and as comfortable as he could be; the sanctuary was in good health; we had money in the bank and improvements were being made all the time; and I had my friends. There was so much that was positive, and seeing Princess always reminded me of that. She went wild when she saw me, dragging herself over, her tongue hanging out of her mouth, her ears pricked up and her tail wagging furiously.

I stepped into her area and immediately crouched beside her, letting her lick my face all the while protesting that I didn't want to be kissed.

A recent bequest had meant that we would be able to buy a neighbouring piece of land, which would add another four acres onto the site, a fact that cheered me immensely. It would mean more space for our existing animals, and the ability to take in even more. That meant more neglected or unwanted beasts could live out their lives in dignity here, even more abandoned animals could be left here, their last chance at finding a loving home. Yet not all of those that deserved a forever family got one. It was a sad truth that some of our loveliest, most deserving, adorable dogs and cats were somehow left here, and would never be rehomed. There didn't seem to be any reasonable explanation, apart from an animal, like Princess, with an obvious disability. Some creatures were just meant to stay with us, or that's how I chose to see it.

'Come on, girl, let's get out and see what's new at the sanctuary. The lads will be in for their morning break soon, so we'll have the land to ourselves.' I placed a dog coat on Princess and waited as she limped a little along the concrete before sliding her bottom back down along the floor.

'Come on, slowcoach, it's jolly chilly out there today.' I felt uplifted by the sight of the bleak and beautiful countryside. Every day I thanked God for letting me live on this twelve-acre patch of the Sussex landscape. Walking round it was almost like a meditation for me; it centred me back into what was real and reminded me who I was in times of crisis.

'There have been many times of crisis, Princess, I promise you. We've been on the verge of bankruptcy so many times I can't count. I had to sell my car and stop my life insurance to pay for fencing, but that was years ago,' I chuckled.

'I never missed not having a car. You can get used to anything, rather like you with that damaged leg, eh, girl?' Princess's ears pricked up as I spoke to her, and even though it must've been very cold on her behind, she stopped momentarily to cock her head to one side, as if to say, 'What now, Mummy?'

'Then there was Peter dying . . .' I paused, as there was no point in raking back over old coals. 'So, yes, there have been a few bad things that have happened, but we got through them, Princess, just as you have so bravely got through your injuries.' Princess was struggling along slowly in her strange hobbling fashion. I waited for her at the pathway that led down to the right to the fields and pastures, looking around. A crow croaked in one of the ash trees behind me, the sheep baaa-ed. One of the peacocks, which had been given to us by a rich local couple who had bought them having no idea of the noise they made, screeched from the top of the bungalow roof where he liked to sit.

A squirrel was scratching at the bark of a tree and I sighed with deep contentment. Whenever I had difficulties or challenges to face, I gained solace from my land and my animals. Watching Princess fight onwards, limping and shuffling to catch up with me, filled me with pride for her. At least she tried. At least she persevered and made an effort to go for walks. I saw her courage and her determination, both qualities I have needed in abundance over the years running this place, and in my heart I saluted her. She, of all the dogs and cats in this place, deserved a good home, and it was the one thing I couldn't give him.

Princess had caught up. She looked up at me and I rustled in my fleece pocket for a dog treat that I threw to her. Deftly, she caught it in her mouth, and crunched loudly as we walked on. The November air was cold, a mist rolling in over the valley from the coast. The trees were bare, the hedgerows brown. It was the kind of day that was made for being indoors, yet I took a visceral pleasure in being outside amid the bleakness of the countryside winter.

The gloom of the day echoed my thoughts as we continued onwards, reaching the horses' paddock at last. None of the bays were standing in the field and were instead sheltering inside the large outbuilding built to house them.

The grass was damp, and a couple of times, Princess slipped as we walked.

'Let's go and see the pigs. The horses aren't available for a visit today.'

The pigsties were directly adjacent to the horses, with a large open field spanning the northernmost part of the sanctuary. We currently had a few sheep grazing there, and even they were ignoring us, although they emitted an occasional baaa to let us know they were still there.

'Their padding will keep them dry,' I said out loud, though of course I had no one but Princess for company.

We stood for a while next to the sties, which were curved sheets of rippled corrugated iron hammered into the ground, each with its own fenced area for the pig to root around in. We had a large saddleback in the first pen, with its big black body with the distinctive white band around it. His name was Eric, and would've been bred to make bacon and pork chops, but had been abandoned in a farmer's field. We had no idea why, and yet again, it was a member of the public who'd spotted him and rung the sanctuary. We currently had nine pigs, so many of them were sharing sties. According to Dan it had become fashionable for small landowners, or those with smallholdings, to buy micropigs. Unfortunately, many unscrupulous breeders were passing off 'normal-sized' pigs as micro ones when they were piglets, and as soon as they started to grow into their massive adult size, they would find they couldn't care for them, and so they were being brought here in ever-increasing numbers.

I looked past the pens to the boundaries of the land. Some of the lads were working on new fencing and building new sheds to house the cows, sheep and goats over the winter. I could hear their shouts and whistles, the blare of the radio as they worked, and it was a comforting sound; newness and creation in the midst of everything else that was crumbling around me. I knew that Dad had mere days left. He was dying, and I had to prepare myself, just as I'd had to do for Peter in the last weeks of his life.

I was more experienced with grief now; I understood how it worked, how it rolled over you and knocked you over sometimes and left you flailing in its wake, and how sometimes it was a beautiful thing, made of sadness and love for the person. Yet still I feared it. I was scared that I would not be strong enough to get through the hours and weeks after my father's passing. I knew how much pain there would be, and I honestly wasn't sure if I had it in me to deal with it this time round. Losing my brother had been bad enough. Losing my father on top of that was almost inconceivable, and yet it was a reality that was creeping closer and closer with each minute that passed.

'Walk on,' I said to Princess, who had become an obedient dog, limping along by my side.

Princess had grown big in the months she'd been with us. She'd grown into the classic boxer body shape with her sloping back, regal upright position and keen, intelligent personality. I couldn't understand how all the people who came to look at her couldn't see what a beautiful dog she was, but I accepted it was part of God's plan for her.

'You keep struggling on, no matter what life has thrown at you,' I murmured, making Princess's head bob up and her tail give an exploratory wag.

She was moving more swiftly as we circled the paddock where the ponies and goats were kept, then turned left to head back to the kennels, past the FIV zone, the cattery and the extended cattery hospital.

'Yes, you just keep going, however difficult and painful it is for you, however hard it is to keep falling over, to keep being rejected, you always keep going. You've inspired me, lovely girl. When things get really hard, as they are about to, I will think of you and your sheer perseverance, and I know I'll get through somehow.' My voice was cracking as a rush of emotion threatened to overtake me. I sat down on one of newly donated benches by the cattery and took a moment to feel the swell of the grief that was hovering ahead, to breathe in the warm doggy smell of Princess, and let the feelings come.

If Princess could overcome her terrible injury, the neglect she'd obviously experienced in order to become the sweet-natured, trusting hound that she was, then I could cope with whatever life was about to throw at me too.

We had navigated the mounds and slopes of the land together, admittedly at a snail's pace, but we'd managed it, and I knew whatever terrain life threw at us from now on, we would do exactly the same: keep our heads down and limp onwards into the uncertain future.

SEVENTEEN

Peaceful Passing

Dad's GP had been in to see him.

'It's not looking good,' he said, shaking his head.

'How long has he got?' I answered, straight to the point as usual.

The doctor hesitated. 'We never know for sure, but I would guess a couple of days at most. He's unconscious most of the time, and he doesn't appear to know where he is or who we are. A few days at most . . .'

The GP, a man in his fifties, looked at me with genuine concern.

'Thank you, doctor. I'll make sure he's as comfortable as possible and I'll stay with him night and day from now on. I couldn't bear it if he died alone,' I said quietly, turning to Di who, as ever, was by my side, supporting me as only a great friend does.

'You don't have to worry about anything, Barby. The Christmas Bazaar is out of your hands. We all know what we're doing. There's literally nothing for you to do outside of caring for him.'

I smiled at her gratefully. Di smiled back. Her face, always pink with exertion or the effect of being outside in all weathers, shone, her blonde hair in tendrils under her woolly hat. She hadn't taken her muddy wellies off and had trailed dirt along the corridor all the way to Dad's room, but I couldn't begrudge her that. She was my oldest friend, the person I turned to in my hours of need, and here she was again, by my side.

'Well, if that's everything . . . I'll leave this prescription. These will make life easier for him until it's time.' The GP packed up his doctor's bag and headed to the front door. By now he knew his way out without having to be told.

Di picked up the green slip and glanced at it. 'I'll head into Sidley to get these for him. Why don't you take a few minutes to yourself?'

'Alright, dearest, and thank you again. I don't know what I'd do without you,' I said, sitting on the chair next to Dad's bedside. He looked tiny now, shrivelled and pale, a shadow of the man he once was.

I waited until we were alone, rubbing his right hand softly, taking care not to hurt his fragile skin. I whispered, 'I'll be here. You won't have to worry about a thing. I'll be by your side, Dad.'

His breaths were rasping, and it looked like he was exerting himself with each inhalation.

'It won't be long now, then you'll be free of pain and free of this. You can look down on us and keep us safe from heaven, and one day we'll all see you up there . . . Just imagine how many animals will greet you on Rainbow Bridge,' I added, wiping away a tear almost angrily. My father was still alive yet I was behaving like he'd already died.

How could he leave me? We'd been together for most of my life, and now he was about to go, forever. My only consolation was our belief in Rainbow Bridge, a place that exists just this side of heaven. It is a place with rolling fields and meadows for all our special animal friends to wait to join whomever they left behind on this plane. Here, upon the death of the owner, pet and human are reunited, and make the walk into heaven, over the bridge together. I knew one day that I'd find Dad there, surrounded by the menagerie of animals he rescued, waiting for me to pass over. It soothed me to think we might be united in death, though it didn't make the pain of him passing any easier to bear right now.

I continued speaking, suddenly realising there was a little soul I needed to talk to before this last phase of Dad's life played out.

'There's something I must do before I join you properly. I won't be long, Dad. Look, I'll leave the television on so you've got company and I'll be back within half an hour at the most.'

He didn't respond. His mouth was half open all the time, his eyelids fluttering as he lay there. He may have understood every word, at least I liked to think so, though the reality was that he was probably halfway between this world and the next, in a kind of quiet delirium.

I held a swab stick to his lips to moisten them with water, then put his hand back down on the familiar sheets.

I had made a decision to concentrate exclusively on Dad, and that meant handing Princess over to Fran. who was overseeing the kennels. It sounds daft, but I wanted to explain to the dog what was happening. I'm a great believer in telling animals what is going on, even though there is no real understanding. It strikes me as respectful to them as creatures of this earth, to include them in decision-making. As I said, it's just me being silly, but I did it every time.

'Princess, it's time to care for my dad now. I'm entrusting you with Fran. You'll be in the best possible hands.' At that, Princess licked my hand as if she understood every word.

I gave her a last cuddle, and a kiss, and I knew it was time to leave.

'Don't worry, Barby. Seriously, she'll be fine. She won't get lonely, and I'll make sure someone's with her all the time,' Fran reassured me.

'Thank you,' I said, holding onto the ledge as I got up from my crouching position.

I didn't look back as I left. I knew the sight of Princess's big brown eyes and funny head, which was always cocked sideways, would make me crumble inside.

Back inside the house, the place was empty. Diane had obviously radioed the volunteers and told them to keep away out of respect. It was a kind gesture, and yet again I marvelled at how this wonderful person had come to be in my life.

Looking down at the other wonderful person, my beloved father, I felt the love I had for him magnify, fill the room, the sky, the fields and the heavens. I loved him devotedly, and he, in turn, had bequeathed me his love for animals, my real inheritance.

My vigil had begun.

All day I stayed close, wiping his brow with cold flannels, swabbing his chapped and cracking lips with moisture. A couple of times, he tried to say something. I had to bend my head down to his lips, but all I could make out was 'Barby . . .' through his laboured breathing.

'Don't try to speak, Dad. Save your strength. I'll be here through the night. Princess is in safe hands with Fran. Did I tell you that I've stopped advertising her for fostering in the newsletter?'

I didn't wait for a response. I kept up my chatter, telling him how we'd tried so many times to find a forever home for the boxer but how we'd failed time and time again. Dad knew all this stuff but I liked telling him again; it helped me to come to terms with my failure to find the lovely dog a home.

'Why don't I read to you? Let's try *If Only They Could Talk* by James Herriot again. You love that book. After all, you've only read it a hundred times so why not once more, eh?'

I leaned over to Dad's rather sparse bookcase. He was never a big reader but what he did read centred on his favourite subject: animals of all kinds.

I shared his pleasure in the novels based on a fictional vet and the pets and owners he encountered. We'd watched *All Creatures Great and Small* together when it was aired on television as it was based on the books, and it had given both Dad and I great pleasure over the years. It was a fitting tribute to return to those stories in his final hours, to share them together again, and to feel sure that he was listening to every word as I read late into the night.

The next day passed in the same way. I felt as though I'd aged twenty years after dozing for a few hours in the armchair next to him.

'I'm as stiff as a board,' I said aloud as I awoke and stretched.

Harry was free to wander about the house, and he had loyally spent the night sleeping on the floor beside us. He gave a great yawn and stretched out his large spaniel body before loping off to the kitchen.

'Do you want your breakfast, dearest? Alright, I'm coming.'

I got up and headed to the kitchen. I hadn't even got changed out of my work clothes and I'm sure I must've looked an absolute fright. I poured the hot water straight from the urn into a teapot and added several teabags. I liked a good strong cuppa first thing. I busied myself making breakfast: my usual of baked beans on toast with a sliced tomato, and toast with marmalade for Dad in the hopes of getting him to eat something. Harry wolfed down his food in thirty seconds then, with a slight wag of his tail, headed outside to find someone to play with.

Carrying the tray back into the bedroom, I caught a glimpse of the rain falling in sheets against the window. It was mid-November, and the night had been stormy. Several times I'd woken up because of a loud gust of wind or the sound of rain falling heavily on the low annexe roof.

'It's going to be a long winter. I hope the lads have finished those new outbuildings. We can't risk our stores of winter feed and hay for the animals getting destroyed by the rain, so we're building proper places to keep them. The prices of feed have sky-rocketed over the last year.'

I wasn't sure if it was Dad or myself I was talking to by now.

'Knock, knock.' Di peered round the doorway. 'I see you've got your breakfast. I was going to ask but as you're tucking in nicely, I don't have to bother!'

I raised an eyebrow and kept on chewing.

'How is he?' she asked. 'Did he have a good night?'

'Well, I think he did but I certainly didn't,' I quipped. 'I've got bloody neck ache from this chair. It isn't the comfiest place to sleep.'

'I could ask the others and see if anyone's got a camp bed you can borrow?' Diane offered.

I felt instantly guilty. My needs were completely secondary to my father's. So what if I had a cricked neck? It was him who was dying, not me.

'Sorry, I didn't mean to make a fuss,' I said, rather shame faced. 'I'm a bit tired. No, we don't need anything, dearest. When I've finished giving Dad his breakfast, I'll try and give him a little wash with a flannel and change him out of his pyjamas into a clean pair.'

'Well, if you need a hand, just buzz me over the walkie-talkie, especially if you need a hand lifting him. I'm a tough old bird.'

She certainly was. Di was a stalwart, a solid, dependable woman who was happy to lug heavy weights without any complaint.

'Er, so what about Princess? Have you spoken to Fran yet? Is she missing me?' I shouted after her as she disappeared down towards the office.

'Not yet. I'm sure Princess is fine. You wouldn't normally have seen her overnight anyway, so why on earth would you think she's missing you already?' Di shouted back at me, making me grumble into my beans.

'She'll know I'm not around,' I said, defensively.

Dad stirred, which made me drop all thoughts of the three-legged dog.

'Are you okay, Dad? Can you hear me?' He said

nothing, just gave a long sigh then settled back down into his sleep.

'Are you still with me, Dad?' I said. I couldn't keep the note of pleading out of my voice.

I put my hand on his chest to check he was breathing, and was gratified to feel the slow movement.

'Still here,' I said tenderly.

I washed him and managed to change his night clothes. I couldn't bear the thought of him lying in dirty pyjamas. The day passed, and by nightfall, I'd exhausted my conversation about the sanctuary. Instead, I wandered into memories from my past; good memories of the animals we looked after and the times we spent together caring for them.

'I'll never forget the day you turned up with that monkey. My goodness, that was a surprise, even for you. You'd only just moved into my flat when you did that. That monkey used to love me giving it a bath in a trug in the garden. And do you remember building him a huge cage in the lounge? I think it had more room than us by the time you'd finished with the wooden frame and chicken wire. He had virtually a whole tree in there, with branches to play on. He was happy as anything. Lord, and there was the bushbaby as well, though I think that came a little later.

'You made Mum furious, but then you knew that anyway. I think that was half the fun for you,' I chuckled. 'Gosh, she was scary when she stood there, her hands on her hips, her eyes blazing, screaming at you. She was a sight to behold, yet it never stopped you bringing strays home.

'I don't know how you had the nerve to bring back all those exotic creatures to a woman who hated animals. It was either very brave of you or very stupid. I think your love for them overrode every other consideration, and I'm so glad it did. Some of the best memories I have were when we would sit in the garden, cleaning out a rabbit's hutch, or brushing a stray dog's fur. They were my happiest times, in fact.'

The memories seemed to blur and I realised I was crying. Tears streamed down my face and I let them come. As night drew in, as the rain ceased and the wind dropped, I was left without words, without anything else left to say. I just had to wait.

Waking suddenly, my heart felt like it was hammering in my chest. I stared around, realising I'd managed to doze off for most of the night, then looked over at Dad. I stared for a moment, coming round from my slumber, and in that moment, I knew.

I stood up, the blankets falling from my lap onto the ground. Like a zombie, I moved towards Dad's bed, my head still thick with sleep, my mind sharpening up with each step I took.

I felt Dad's hand. It was still warm, but I knew.

I placed my hand gently on his chest. There was no movement. I heard no rasping breath. He must have passed away mere seconds earlier, and it was pure intuition that had awoken me.

Time seemed to freeze. I stood and looked at Dad's face as it drained of colour, as his hands began to cool, and he lay there, still as stone. My beloved father had died. The world had changed utterly, and he had left me at last.

I carefully placed his hands onto his chest and pulled the blanket up, a small gesture to prepare him for what was to come next.

I wasn't ready to tell anyone yet, and so I sat back down, pulling my chair as close to the bed as I could, and listened to the silence that was interrupted now and then by a low noise from the animals.

Dawn hadn't risen, and when it did, I knew I would have to acknowledge the passing of the man I loved with all my heart. There was a stillness in the room, and for a moment, I didn't feel sadness; I felt the joy of knowing he'd gone to a better place. I knew my grief would come, rolling over me like thunder across the fields. The grief was hovering at my shoulder, waiting, waiting for me to greet it like an old friend.

'You've done this before, Barby, with Peter,' I told myself. 'You got through it, and you'll get through this . . .'

I don't know if I believed my own words. I just knew that I'd lost the best person of my life, my greatest solace, my heart and soul. He had drifted away like smoke on the breeze, and I would never, ever see his dear face again, or hear his echo of 'You there?' as he walked into the house.

He was gone.

The feelings broke like a dam. I felt suddenly engulfed by a raw pain that exploded inside me. He was gone. He was gone. He was gone.

How would I live without him?

EIGHTEEN

Life Without Dad

After the flurry of people who'd come to the house – the GP, the undertaker, the well-wishers – I found myself longing for solitude to mourn my father properly, in my own private space and time.

The funeral was a small affair, attended mostly by my motley crew from the sanctuary, as well as my younger sister Pam.

I hated dwelling on things, and even during the service, I wanted it to be over, for my father's ashes to be brought to me to bury on my land so we would be together in spirit.

When, eventually, I was handed a plain box filled with a bag containing my father's remains, I couldn't really believe it was him.

I couldn't face sorting through his things, yet I had to do it. I packaged up his clean clothes to give away, his few possessions staying mostly with me, including his small pocket radio, a few books and his comb.

I went through the motions at work, ringing food suppliers, calling businesses for their donations as the bazaar was nearly upon us, working outside long into each evening, though it was December and the harsh winter winds cut through me like slivers of ice. I didn't want any time to think, yet I yearned to find a place of solitude to unpack my grief. It wasn't logical. My emotions were like a roller-coaster. I cried for days after Dad's death, and even the sight of Princess, who had been wild with happiness at seeing me again, couldn't lift my despair.

Living without my father was something I knew I'd have to learn to do, one day. That day had come, yet I had no idea how to do it. I hadn't prepared at all. How could I? How could I have imagined what it would be like without him, and how desperately alone I would feel?

I think that's why I threw myself into the chores and jobs of the sanctuary. I had to fend off the aching sadness somehow, and I did it as I always do, with work, work and more work.

Even Harry, the grumpy old thing, sensed the change in me. He took to following me about, sitting next to me as I wept into my sodden handkerchief, and lying next to me on my bed at nights, which he hadn't done since Princess had appeared. Night times were the worst, and Harry was an absolute darling. He kept me company as I cried through each night, dozing off only fitfully through the long, dark hours. I still kept thinking I could hear my dad saying 'You there?' from the darkness, though my rational mind knew this couldn't be so.

It was a wilderness of emotions. I felt overwhelmed, in turn exhausted then energised to the point of overworking, before collapsing each evening to spend the next few hours sobbing for my lovely father.

I'd grieved for my brother, but this was on a different scale. Dad had been the most dependable person in my life. He had been my rock, and I was only just beginning to understand how much his quiet, gentle presence had centred and grounded me in the work I did and the life I led. Without him, everything seemed to have lost its meaning. At times I wondered if I was going crazy as I even questioned my own passion for animals, thinking I only loved them to be closer to Dad. Luckily, I had good friends who saw me through those first, awful weeks when the grief made me half mad.

'You're going to be okay, Barby. What you're thinking is perfectly natural. You're grieving, that's all. It's pure grief for someone you loved dearly,' Di said one evening when I told her about the thoughts I'd been having. As I have mentioned, after I lost Teddy, I'd even thought about walking away from the sanctuary, I was so broken-hearted, until Di convinced me that I was mother to more than just Teddy. In fact, I was a mum to all six hundred or so animals that called this place their home. I have never forgotten what she said, and it really helped every time I questioned my love for animals and my mission in life now that Dad was gone.

We currently had cats, dogs, donkeys, goats, rabbits, geese, ducks, chickens, sheep, cows, pigs, a rather forlorn budgie, a cockatiel, guinea pigs, gerbils, pigeons, turkeys, guinea fowl, pheasants, peacocks, Shetland ponies and a horse on site. I couldn't abandon them just because I was stricken by sadness. I had to take Diane's wise words on board and I remembered them now, when I needed them most.

'There have been times when I really thought my life was over and I couldn't go on here,' I said, waving my arm absent-mindedly around the vicinity of the neighbouring field. I was outside mending a fence with Di and Dan.

'You always say that, Barby, but we know you'd never leave this place,' Dan said, hammering a post into the wet earth.

'He's right,' chipped in Diane. 'Now, you watch what you're hitting, Dan, because I'm the one holding this fence post.'

'Don't worry, you'll know if I change my mind about whacking the fence and decide it's your turn.' He grinned. 'Seriously, though, Barby, you need to take some time off over Christmas and allow yourself a bit of room to come to terms with the loss of your dad. I know you work through your problems by overworking, but you've been through a lot,' he finished, hitting the post with a thud.

'Is that sympathy I'm hearing, Dan?' I said, arching an eyebrow.

'Yes, it is, Barby,' Dan said simply.

I looked at him, and the sight of his kind face immediately brought fresh tears to my eyes.

'I'm fine,' I said gruffly, wiping away a tear on the sleeve of my jacket.

'Yes, you look it,' Di said pointedly. 'We know you're a trooper but you need to grieve properly. You'll make yourself ill otherwise.'

I nodded. I knew they were both right. I'd all but stopped sleeping, and I started each day with eyes red-raw from weeping. I was exhausted but I didn't seem able to stop.

'Why don't you leave this? We can manage. Go and see Princess. She's been missing you . . .' Di said gently.

I hadn't been to see her much. Something about her trusting, loyal eyes made me want to cry even harder every time I saw her. Her disability filled me with such feelings of pathos that I just couldn't bear seeing her try to walk any more.

I knew my friends were right, though. I had neglected Princess of late, and it wasn't her fault she looked so tragic.

I walked off, my boots slipping on the muddy soil. We were repairing fencing that had come loose in the end field, the new acres that now housed many of our large farm animals. Winter was the time we fixed things across the site as we didn't have time during the spring and summer because of visitors.

I skirted past the horses and carried on round the back of the kennels, pushing the door open and stamping my feet once inside.

The door to the first pen was open and I peered in to see Fran crouching on the concrete, looking over a cocker spaniel.

'New one?' I said.

Fran looked up at me.

'Hi, Barby, here to see Princess?'

Nodding, I asked: 'Who's this? He looks in a terrible state.'

'Actually, *she's* not as bad as she looks though she has very bad mange.'

'Poor girl,' I said, coming over and crouching next to her. The small dog's skin was sore where she had scratched the skin condition, which is caused by mites. Much of her fur was missing, and what remained was patchy and scraggy.

'Her name is Hooch. She came in this morning, but I didn't like to bother you . . .' Fran was, for once, being very considerate!

'Thank you,' I said, and I really meant it. Normally, I wanted to know everything that went on, every dog that came in, every cat or mouse or hen, but I just couldn't take it in at the moment, and I was grateful for Fran taking over.

'Keep me posted, won't you?' I said as I got up. There was only one dog I wanted to see today, and that was Princess.

'Princess!' I cried as I saw her. She was playing with a squeaky toy that I could hear as I walked into her pen.

Instantly, the dog limped over, tail wagging, tongue lolling out as was her way, and I got slobbered by the drooling, overexcited girl as I knelt next to her. I breathed in her warm, doggie smell, the smell that felt like home to me, and I thanked God for keeping her here until this moment so she could comfort me in my loss.

'Perhaps there was a bigger plan for you, after all,' I said, burying my face in her glossy deep brown fur. Her coat shone and her eyes were liquid happiness as she pretended to gnaw at my hand.

I spent a happy morning with her, and for those few precious hours, I didn't think about my grief, the loss of my father or anything else except living in the moment, as this beautiful animal had taught me to do.

Christmas came and went. I'd tried to ignore it as it only made me feel worse that I couldn't spend it with Dad as I'd done for so many years. The only acknowledgement I gave to the festive season was to light three candles, for Peter, Teddy and Dad, on Christmas afternoon as the day descended into twilight. I shut my door, microwaved a roast dinner and settled down with the television blaring and Harry in his permanent grump beside me. I walked Princess that day, and I really believed that our destiny was set. Princess would live out her days with me at the sanctuary, and even though I felt sad for her, I was glad for her companionship over those bleak first months of the new year.

*

Weeks later, I was sitting opening yet more vet bills, when the phone rang. I'd gasped when I'd seen the amount at the bottom of the latest bill, for Hooch's mange treatment, and was happy to drop it and reach for the receiver.

'Hello, Barby Keel Animal Sanctuary. Can I help you?' I said, casting my eye down the list of numbers and shaking my head.

'Oh yes, my name is Mr Smith. I'm looking for a companion dog.' He had a nice voice, and sounded elderly.

'Right, okay, well we have several that might suit. Do you mean a companion for another dog, or for yourself?' I asked, my mind on the bill, wondering how on earth we would cover it. Just then a thought crossed my mind. I knew of a very caring lady who couldn't keep a pet due to infirmity but she'd offered to sponsor a dog instead. *I wonder if she'd like to sponsor Hooch?* I muttered under my breath.

'What was that, dear? Sorry, my hearing isn't what it used to be,' the gentleman on the other end of the phone said.

'Oh, I'm so sorry. I was miles away. Yes, we have a couple of lovely dogs you are welcome to come and see.'

'Actually, I'd heard about a boxer you have. Am I right in thinkings she has only three legs? I don't mind, I'm just curious. I'd like to come and see her; I have a soft spot for boxers.'

I sighed.

How many times had I heard the same interest from people, only to face their disappointment when they saw her?

'I warn you, she's disabled, can only shuffle and limp at slow speed, and some people find her injury very off-putting,' I said firmly. I didn't want any time-wasters. I had enough on my plate juggling our income and expenses on top of my recent loss.

'That's settled then.' I could hear the man was smiling. 'I'll be over tomorrow afternoon, if I may?' he finished.

'Yes, that's fine, though don't get your hopes up. It will take a very special person to see past Princess's disability,' I said, as much to myself as to the caller.

I was long past feeling excited for the boxer. I knew this would end in rejection, just like all the others, and I think I'd finally got used to seeing it, though I didn't like it.

I was waiting by the gate the next day when Mr Smith pulled up the drive in a hatchback that had seen better days. The elderly gent got out of his car and walked over to me. He used a stick and was limping heavily.

'I can't walk far these days. Hello, I'm very glad to meet you, Miss Keel,' he said politely.

I warmed to him instantly. He had a kind face, not unlike my dad's, with grey wisps of hair, a stooped, slender frame and a smile that was open.

'I'm pleased to meet you too, dear. Come this way. Can I help you or can you manage the paving?' I asked, holding the gate open for him.

He walked slowly round to the kennels and we chatted pleasantly about the sanctuary. He seemed most interested in all aspects of the shelter and was clearly an animal lover.

'Come inside,' I said, pushing the door open for him. It was a mild spring day but there was still a nip in the air and I realised I felt slightly protective of him, even though I'd never met him before.

'So, how did you know about our darling boisterous Princess, then?' I smiled as he limped down to the end pen.

'I saw an advert for her in one of your newsletters. I was lucky that she hadn't been given to someone else. As soon as I saw her, I thought, "That's my dog." Can you believe that?' he chuckled.

I wanted to believe him. He seemed a lovely man, and he clearly adored dogs as he chattered away about pets he'd had in the past.

It was difficult, when people sounded so positive, but for my own sake, and for Princess's, I needed to keep a clear head.

Fran winked at me as I passed, and I raised my eyebrows in response, as if to say, 'Here we go again.'

Finally, we opened the pen, and the two came face to face with each other. Princess was shaking her head as she pretended to ravage a stuffed toy. She stopped what she was doing the instant she saw me, but today, she didn't come straight over to me. Today, she took one look at the elderly gentleman and shuffled her way over to him. Drool was forming in her mouth as she went, her three legs looked comical as they moved in her funny, awkward way towards the visitor, but to my surprise, the man seemed completely unfazed by Princess's appearance. In fact, he seemed delighted to see her. He bent over and, propping his stick against the wall, he ruffled her fur with both hands while crooning to the dog how beautiful she was.

I stood there, gobsmacked. There was no other word for it. I was completely and utterly shocked, in the best way possible.

It's a special chemistry that occurs between a dog and its new owner. To be sure a hound is going to a loving, permanent home, we have to see that spark, the instant bonding that comes when humans and animals are matched perfectly.

I was astounded because I was seeing it happening right in front of my eyes.

I stayed silent, not wanting to ruin the moment. Princess was rolling on the floor, her tail going like the clappers, making excitable noises while Mr Smith was tickling her tummy, stroking the white stripe down her chest and telling her what a brave dog she was.

Minutes passed.

I heard Fran creep up behind me.

'What's going on?' he hissed, and I just looked at him, wide-eyed and beaming with happiness.

'I think they've just found each other,' I whispered, stepping back to leave them to their bonding. I almost felt like I was intruding on their newfound happiness.

I'd never seen Princess make a beeline for a prospective owner. She was usually pleased to see me first before checking out anyone else. She hadn't even glanced at me from the minute she set eyes on the man. The gent was the same. He didn't turn his back. He didn't step back or make excuses, or look elsewhere. He fixed his gaze firmly on the boxer, and greeted her like an old friend.

'No doubt if I leave them for an hour, the gent will get bored or will have found an excuse not to take Princess,' I said to Fran as I walked back to the house, though something inside told me I was wrong this time.

'Tell him to come over when he's ready, and you might need to help him.' Fran nodded.

More than an hour went past. I sat watching the clock, wondering if the chap had left without saying goodbye.

Just then, there was a knock on the door. I opened it to find him standing there, leaning against the doorframe, panting a bit.

'I'll take her,' was all he said.

NINETEEN

Love at First Sight

I stood at the door, staring into the elderly gentleman's smile and then just laughed. 'You don't know how long I've waited to hear those words,' I said at last, making us both smile again.

'I knew from the moment I set eyes on her, in your newsletter, that she was the dog for me. I just knew,' he said.

I nodded. I understood that strange connection that exists, even before meeting an animal. It is an indefinable charge, an attraction that defies words, and the bond that existed already between this man and our lovely Princess was unmistakable.

'You'd better come in then.'

Mr Smith shuffled into the lounge. Even the way he moved reminded me of the dog, the awkward gait, the staccato limp, the slowness and the determination.

'Here, take a seat and I'll go and find the rehoming forms. Back in a sec. Would you like a cup of tea?' My voice drifted through from the office where I was already leafing through a new stack of official documents.

'Oh, where are they? What has Dan done with the forms?' I muttered as I searched.

'Yes please, thank you. I'd love a tea,' came the man's voice.

'My colleague Dan will have to come up and see your home to make sure it's suitable for Princess. Is that okay?' I said as I searched.

'Bingo!' I exclaimed as I pulled the documents from a pile, brandishing them as I marched back to the kitchen. I felt a strange sense of urgency, as if I didn't trust that this would happen so I'd better sign him up quickly.

'That's alright,' Mr Smith replied patiently.

'We'll sort out which day they can come, but first let's get these forms filled in so we can get you sorted,' I said, trying to find a pen for the chap who sat there smiling in the calmest way.

Meanwhile, Dan was in the kitchen, making himself a cup of tea.

'Going well?' he said, putting his head round the door and smiling.

'Yes, we'll see,' I said vaguely. I didn't want to jinx things. I would only celebrate when those papers were signed.

'Would you make him a cuppa while I chat through the checks we need to do?' I murmured. I was feeling jittery, and I realised I wasn't just feeling mistrusting, I was also starting to realise that this meant Princess, my beloved Princess, would also be leaving us.

'Sorry to keep you. Here are some forms for you to fill in. We need to know a few details about you before we can go ahead, subject to the home check, of course,' I explained.

'Right you are. Thank you. I can go through them now?' he asked.

'Please do,' I replied.

Mr Smith really was a very kindly, respectful soul.

I gazed out of my patio doors that looked out onto the rabbit pen with its iron benches out front for visitors to sit on in the summer. Several volunteers were sitting drinking coffee, and gossiping, no doubt!

Fran walked past, typing into his mobile phone, which made me tut. Then Dan walked over and they exchanged a few words. I watched them all, going about their daily business of looking after all the creatures no one wanted. It was a sight that gave me great comfort. *The world keeps turning, and we are all just tiny cogs in a giant wheel*, I thought to myself. Dad might be gone but his spirit was still here on this land. I felt it when I walked out in the still-chilly mornings with Princess or Harry. I felt him when I watched volunteers cheerfully go about their work, expecting nothing in return except the feeling of being of service. I felt him with me as I filed paperwork, ordered animal feed, rang prospective fosterers, and helped clean out the cattery. I felt him when I lay down at night, Harry by my side, Princess asleep in the kennels. I knew he was with me as the seasons slowly changed and winter mellowed into spring. I missed him with all my heart but I knew it had been his time to go. He'd lived a long and mostly happy life, and he'd devoted all of it to helping stray, unwanted and abandoned animals. This sanctuary was as much his legacy as mine because he gave me that passion. Every decision I made, every animal I'd taken in over the years – and they amounted to thousands – was the result of my early years spent with my father, watching his devotion as it became mine.

'Miss Keel? I've finished. I hope I didn't take too long. These days my hands don't write as well as they used to.'

The chap forced me out of my reverie. I pulled my gaze away from the goings-on outside my window, back to the present moment, where the dog without hope was being given her forever home at last.

I felt a lump form in my throat, which I tried to swallow down. It would be hard to let go of the dog I'd come to love as much as any of my mutts, past or present.

'Thank you, that all looks fine,' I said, scanning the pages.

'Dan will be in touch about coming to see your home, and I suggest you come back in a few days and we can go for a walk with Princess. You'll get a better picture of her mobility and overall health that way.'

'That sounds like a good idea, thank you for suggesting it. I'll be back in on Thursday, if that is convenient for you?' he said.

'It is. I look forward to seeing you again,' I replied, showing him the door.

Part of me had already decided that this was the last time we'd ever see the man, even though he was very keen. I wasn't going to raise my expectations before it was all signed and sealed.

A couple of days later, Dan took Princess up to Tunbridge Wells to do the home check. All day I was unable to concentrate, fixating on the thought that it would be disastrous, that Princess would somehow disgrace herself, or the home wouldn't be suitable.

When Dan returned, I almost ran to the kennels to meet them both.

'You okay, Barby?' Dan said in his usual placid way.

'I'm fine, but how did it go?' I panted.

'It couldn't have gone better.' Dan beamed. I stroked Princess as I stared at my co-worker.

'We got there and Princess was perfect. She couldn't have played it any better. It was a really sweet moment.'

'Go on,' I urged him.

'Well, Mr Smith had a terrier that died, which is why he wanted another dog, and so he brought out the dog bed, which was tiny. Princess is obviously a large dog but she went and sat in it, just squeezing her bum into it, then sat there looking like she was saying "please home me".

'It was brilliant. Princess couldn't have been any more charming if she'd tried,' Dan added, reaching down to pet Princess.

'You clever girl!' I smiled and reached into my pocket for a treat. Princess immediately sat upright again, her tail wagging furiously.

I burst into laughter.

'You've learned to be a real heartbreaker,' I exclaimed, delighted with her behaviour, and the wonderful connection that so clearly existed between the dog and her new owner.

'So, we're all set then?' I asked.

Dan nodded. 'He'll be back on Thursday to collect her. Princess has a new home at long last.'

Despite this happy news, I still didn't trust that it would all go smoothly. I'd seen too much disappointment when it came to this dog.

When Thursday, the rehoming day, came, I crept out that morning to explain to Princess that she mustn't be sad if the old chap didn't reappear. I was doing it for myself, of course, but, as usual, Princess seemed to understand every word.

'We all still love you, me especially, so don't you worry if Mr Smith doesn't show up. There are plenty of people here to love you,' I said, wiping away a tear that betrayed my feelings.

She watched me talking. Her intelligent eyes were alert, Her tail wagging. After I'd finished, I gave her a cuddle and, I hate to admit it, but part of me actually wanted her prospective new owner to vanish back where he came from. Princess licked my hand as if she understood and was trying to comfort me.

I spent the rest of the day trying to carry on as usual as there was so much to do. A pig we had rehomed to a retreat was coming back because it had been bullied by the centre's existing pigs, which had upset me greatly, and we had to make arrangements to pick up the poor beast and find somewhere to put him when he returned. Even though there was plenty going on to distract me, I couldn't stop my gaze flicking up to the clock every fifteen minutes or so.

'He'll be here,' said Diane. She could tell I was a mixture of worry and regret.

'He might, or he might not,' I pouted back at my friend, trying to hide how wretched I felt. I hated seeing animals leave us, even if they were going to the loving homes we'd found for them. I loved every animal at the sanctuary, not just the dogs and cats. Every one of them had a place in my heart.

Part of me was thrilled Princess was going and so I was fretting about whether Mr Smith really would be true to his word and come to collect Princess, and part of me was desperately sad, not wanting the hound to go at all, and knowing I'd have to go through the same familiar feelings of loss.

At two o'clock on the dot, Mr Smith's car pulled slowly into the driveway. I was sitting in my chair looking over at the large television screen that flicked between different security camera viewpoints. I eased myself up out of my chair, and was quickly replaced by Henrietta, the chicken who adored football.

She'd appeared inside my house one day at the start of spring, and seemed in no hurry to leave, no matter how many times she was shooed out. In the end, I'd given up trying to make her live outside with the other chickens. The only problem was, she liked my favourite armchair to roost in, so she would sit there all day, while I perched on the edge in front of her.

The funniest thing was that I discovered she was a football fan. I was watching a game with Manchester United, my favourite team, and when a goal was scored, Henrietta started to flap her wings and cluck loudly. Thinking it was a coincidence, I made sure she was present when I had other matches on, but it was only Manchester United that she got excited about. The staff had started to call her David Peckham, and I'd even had a small chicken-sized footie scarf made for her to wear.

'Well, Henrietta, it seems I was wrong about the elderly chap. That's definitely his car. Stop flapping, I'm going!' I laughed as Henrietta showed me I was getting in the way of her brooding.

I met Mr Smith at the gate and this time Fran came to greet us both, with Princess limping behind him. I was cheered to see how the dog now mostly limped on her three legs rather than bottom-shuffled, as I called it. Over time, her confidence had grown, and so had the strength in her remaining limbs.

She wobbled furiously at times, but she kept going, and the sight of her made all three of us stop and grin.

'Good girl,' said the elderly man. 'That looks like it is as much of a struggle for you as for me.'

Fran had put a nice new black collar on her with a shiny metal disc with her name on. 'I left the other side empty where the phone number should be as I wasn't sure which number to put.'

'Thank you, Fran, that's sensible. Now, shall we go for a walk?'

I led the elderly man, with his stick and his limp, through the sanctuary down to the bottom fields. The hedgerows were starting to burst with blossom and that fresh new green of spring. The day was breezy and there had been a light rain shower earlier, making the scent of the grass, trees and plants sing in the sunlight.

It wasn't easy going, and I started to wonder if I should've just taken the two of them down the lane that dissected the fields, as it would've been an easier journey.

'There's a gate down here. We can reach the road there and it should be easier to walk. Is that okay?' I called to them. Both were struggling along, though they both looked happy to be outside amidst the beauty of the countryside.

Their pleasure in each other's company hadn't dimmed. If anything, they looked even more besotted with each other than they had the first time I'd seen them together. The pair trotted and walked at a similar pace, Mr Smith chatting away to Princess while the dog appeared to hang on every word.

I could've laughed out loud with delight, yet a part of me was devastated at the prospect of seeing this lovely dog go. She was truly a part of the fabric of the sanctuary. Everyone knew her, and knew of her struggles. She had been with us for two years by now, and I marvelled at the change in her from the desperately frightened and ill puppy that had been dumped on our doorstep. She had learned to hobble on her three legs but it had taken many months, and many tumbles to get to this point. I knew that it wouldn't ever get easier for her. In the end, her remaining limbs would weaken as she grew older and would be unable to support her. That thought made me shudder. It was imperative that she had found a home, a loving place that would care for her and support her as time went on. I couldn't believe that time had come, after everything she'd been through.

'Let's head back, I think there's another shower imminent,' I said, peering up to the skies. A large grey cloud had moved overhead, threatening rain at any moment.

The first fat drops were falling as we reached the kennels. Princess shook the moisture off herself, for a moment forgetting she was missing a leg, and promptly tipped over. This time, it wasn't me who came to Princess's aid, but the elderly man. It was heartening to see how affectionate he was with the dog. He helped her back up, tutting at the weather and stroking her lovely glossy fur.

I had seen that it was love at first sight when these two met, and I was glad to see that the love had remained and that Princess had found her forever home in the form of this sweet gentleman.

I left the pair together to say goodbye and wandered back to the bungalow to carry on with my workload. My heart felt light as a feather as I went, and I felt like whistling though I've never been able to hold a tune in my life.

I settled down, looking around my room, covered in statues of meerkats, which were my current obsession after a well-known advert had appeared on television. I knew I was a rather eccentric lady, and I didn't care a jot. I loved animals, darts and meerkats, in that order!

Henrietta was making broody noises from my armchair so I left her in peace and went out to the kitchen to begin the daily job of cleaning the trays of eggs gathered fresh from the chickens. It never failed to annoy me that people wouldn't see past a bit of straw and chicken poo when they bought fresh eggs, but the ladies in the shop we ran in Bexhill said they sold far more when they had been cleaned of the natural detritus.

I stood at the sink, looking out over the undulating fields and valleys I called home, along with the six hundred other residents of various species. I hummed as I worked, washing the eggs and carefully patting them dry. It was just another day at the Barby Keel Animal Sanctuary.

TWENTY

Forever Home

I woke suddenly as if jolted by an alarm clock. I'd never had need of one, of course, as I had several cockerels who were a perfectly adequate substitute; waking me from four in the summer and as late as six in the winter.

I looked over at my clock. It was almost five o'clock, and, as if on cue, the cock-a-doodle-doos started amid the first murmurings of the dawn chorus.

Sunlight streaked the sky as night turned to day, and I realised with a knot of sadness in my stomach that today was the day Princess would leave us at last.

Harry was snoozing next to me. He hated waking up early, and often in the summer, I'd be up and about before him, getting on with the tasks in hand until the lazybones dog roused himself. This morning, though, he gave a long sigh, opening one beady eye as if to check what I was up to as I eased myself out of bed, then shut it again, determined to carry on sleeping.

'You are a naughty dog, I don't know why I bothered to take you in. Oh, don't wag your tail at me. I know you. You're only interested in snoozing and food.'

Harry shifted his great weight, his tail making a thudding sound against the bed as he wagged it.

'I'm getting up because today is the day that our gorgeous girl, Princess, is leaving us.' Even as I said the words out loud, I couldn't quite believe they were true. I knew the feelings of losing her would hit me later, but now it all seemed rather unreal.

'After breakfast, I'm going to make the most of my time left with her to take her out. Our last walk together . . .' Even that sounded strange. I'd tried to find Princess a home so many times. So many people had let her down and rejected her, or backed off, that it felt like this day would never come.

It has come though, Barby, I thought, *and you'd better make the most of it or you'll regret it forever if you don't say goodbye to her properly.*

'See you soon, Harry. You know you can join us if you decide to get up at all today,' I called to the sleeping hound as I walked into the kitchen.

Di was already there, sitting at the table, munching on a piece of toast.

'I thought I could smell burned toast.' I grinned, grabbing a cup from the top cupboard and a teabag from the pot. I poured hot water into the mug and plonked myself down at the table.

'Here have a slice,' Di said companionably, offering me a piece.

'I don't mind if I do, thank you, dearest,' I said, taking one.

Biting into the crumbly bread, slathered with butter, I looked over at my friend.

'Big day today . . .' Di didn't need to say anything more. She knew me so well. She knew I'd be struggling to come to terms with Princess's departure, and that I wouldn't truly show my feelings until after she'd gone.

'Big day,' I echoed. 'I'm going to take Princess out for a walk, just me and her.'

I didn't have to explain why. Diane knew that when animals left us, it was an emotional experience for me and for all of the staff.

So many of us had watched Princess's trials and tribulations, her terrible amputation, her slow recovery, her blossoming into the lovable, boisterous dog she was today. We'd all witnessed her rejection time and time again, and how it never defeated her. She always bounced back, always greeted us with joy and mischief, and she'd repaid our care of her a million times over with her sheer resilience and affectionate nature.

'Princess is a dog in a thousand. She's special, and we've been so lucky to have her here. I didn't think an animal, treated with neglect and then injured so badly, would survive with her love of life intact, and yet Princess did just that.' Di nodded as I spoke.

'She's a sweet thing,' she agreed.

'She's dear to all of us. How will we let her go?' I asked, suddenly downcast.

There was silence for a moment, then Di said, 'Because we have to . . .'

She was right, of course.

We had to let her go because she needed a home, a bed to call her own, a new owner to devote themselves to her. However much we loved Princess, we'd always known that rehoming was the right option for her.

'Over time her legs will deteriorate. She'll need lots of love and lots of patience, and the chap who's coming for her has those in spades,' Di added.

I put my toast down.

'I need to go and see her. In a funny way, she's felt like mine for the time she's been here. I feel like I'm giving away *my* dog.' I felt an instant contraction in my heart. I didn't want Princess to go. I knew I would be devastated at another loss, even though this one was for the best. Logic played no part in my feelings. My head knew this was right, though my heart would pine for this girl for a long time to come.

'Go, Barby. Have your breakfast when you get back. Mr Smith won't be arriving until mid-morning, so you still have some time.'

I reached the kennels a few moments later. Fran was there, along with a couple of young people who couldn't have been long out of their teenage years.

'Hello, I'm Barby,' I said as I entered.

'Still haven't learned to knock,' joked Fran. He was holding Hooch still while the girl gently inspected his fur.

'How's the mange?' I asked, reaching down to give the spaniel a quick stroke.

'It's starting to heal. We've noticed some bits of skin that seem less sore, though it'll be a long journey to get her right again. Unbelievable that dogs come here in that condition,' Fran said, shaking his head. 'I don't know what happens to people to make them lose sight of their pet. It took a while for the infestation to get this bad, so it's not like they didn't have warning,' he added.

'You'd think they'd ask for help sooner if they couldn't afford the vet bills. Why let an animal suffer needlessly?' I didn't understand the actions of people. Why keep a pet if you couldn't afford it or couldn't look after it? I knew that circumstances changed, people lost their jobs or were put on zero-hour contracts, but something like mange would have taken a while to establish itself, and there would've been time to get the right treatment.

Fran shrugged. 'It's a mystery why we get half the animals we do. I don't understand either.'

We both stood and looked at Hooch. She seemed a friendly, happy enough dog, though she was always scratching, which made her skin condition worse and prolonged her treatment.

'She's in the best hands.' I smiled.

'Blimey, Barby, is that a compliment? I don't think I've ever had one of those from you, you old witch!'

I managed to laugh at that.

'I'm not myself today. It's Princess's last day and it's really got to me. I can't bear it when animals leave, and she has been with us for so long, it felt like she was my dog.'

Fran nodded but didn't reply. He knew how it felt to let go of a beloved animal, especially one we'd cared for and nursed back to health. It was a wrench, but part of the emotional rollercoaster that was part and parcel of working in a rescue shelter.

'It's not something that will ever change, Barby,' he said. 'There will be more dogs, more cats, more animals every day that need our love. Princess is one of hundreds that have passed through here, and they won't stop coming.'

I looked at him.

'I know, Fran, but it has never stopped me from falling in love with them, time and time again. And I'm pretty sure I won't ever change.' It was my turn to shrug.

'We all do our best for the creatures that find themselves here, and for the time they're with us they become part of the family. I cried for days after a duck was run over on our driveway. It had got out through the gate and I was so cross that one of the volunteers could be so careless. It doesn't matter to me if it's a duck, a dog, a mouse or a peacock. They're all special.'

'And I know a dog that's extra special, one that is being

rehomed today. Don't waste any more time with us. Go and take Princess out. The man will be here in a couple of hours . . .'

Princess was by the entrance to her pen, having heard my voice.

When I opened the door, she tried to get up, her tail beating against the floor while she tried to leap up to smother me with kisses.

'Down, girl, that's it. I don't want you falling over again, you silly girl,' I said, beaming with joy at the gift of this dog's happiness at seeing me.

'Today is a very special day. It's the day you get a proper daddy and a home of your own. Dan has been to check it out and he says it's perfect for you: a bungalow, so there are no stairs, with a garden on one level. We couldn't have found a better match for you. Are you coming with me for a last walkies?' As I said it, that damned frog reappeared in my throat, choking my words.

The tears were already there, welling up in my eyes at the sight of this dog, one I'd grown to love fiercely.

'We'll have a nice morning together, just you and me, and we'll say goodbye to the sanctuary that has been your home for so long.'

Princess didn't need much encouragement. She limped out, stopping to sniff at Hooch on her way and to get a few cuddles and strokes from Fran and his team.

I shooed them off, not wanting to waste a moment with the dog who had stolen my heart, and, together, we made

233

it outside. It was a lovely spring day. The air was mild, the breeze gentle, though the sun sometimes disappeared behind the clouds. In short, it was the perfect day to walk out for the last time with Princess.

We struck out past the paddocks and into the large expanse of field that spanned the bottom end of the site. The sheep ignored us after realising that it wasn't feeding time, and we came to a stump left after a tree was felled.

'Perfect place for a sit-down,' I said to Princess, who was limping along after me. Occasionally, she tried to run and mostly ended up flat on her face but it never stopped her. I'd brought a ball out to the field to give him something to chase at her own speed and, once she'd caught up, I threw it in a large arc. Princess instantly focused, limping off in the right direction.

'Good girl!' I smiled. 'Fetch!'

A few moments later, she returned with the ball in her drooling mouth.

'Urgh, you boxers are terrible ones for dribbling. The ball is soaked.' I held it gingerly between two fingers and threw it again, this time in the opposite direction.

Off she went again, knowing instantly where it had landed though she was slow to get there to retrieve it.

I wiped my fingers on my jumper, and looked around me. The sight of this land never failed to amaze me. In winter it was bleak and muddy underfoot, with lingering mists that sat in the valleys for days, and bare trees that reached spiky fingers into the grey skies. In summer it was green and lush, with wild flowers at the far edges, grass that needed cropping regularly as it grew so quickly, and sunbaked soil.

Spring and autumn were my favourite seasons, though. Spring was fresh with the awakening of the earth and plants after each dismal winter, and I loved the sense of renewal as the trees burst back into life and the hedgerows sang with the activities of birds making nests.

Autumn was a mellow month. The trees dropped their leaves with languid beauty after a display of browns, oranges and reds to rival any fireworks night. I knew we were blessed to live here, to have the space, though more and more animals arrived each day to fill it.

I watched as Princess limped back. She was a little slower this time, and I saw it didn't take much to tire her out.

'Come and sit with me for a while,' I said, patting the edge of the tree stump. 'We can play ball later.'

'Let me tell you about my dad. Now you're going to get a new daddy, while I've just lost mine.

'Mine was a loving soul, a man who didn't really care for company except for other animal lovers. He worked on every bit of this land. He built some of the fences up there,' I said, turning my face to the sun and looking back at the perimeter fencing around the paddock.

'He loved the pigs, and I often saw him standing against the sties watching them and giving them stale bread as a treat. He created my garden for me, making me a little fountain and a pond, and chose the flowers that are growing there. He did so much for us here. He loved this place, and we loved him. We loved him for his simplicity and his kind-heartedness. You were lucky, Princess, you knew him too, for a while . . .' I drifted off. The sun had come out and was warming my face, which I held up to meet it.

Over time, grief changes though it never goes away. I'd lost my father and there would always be a gap in my heart, but I also knew that he was here with me in spirit. On days like this, with the sun shining and the new smell of grass, heavy still with dew, I could feel him in the wind, in the soil where I planted my feet, and in the very heart of this magical place.

'Princess, today you are leaving me too.' I leaned in for a cuddle, fearing my emotions would overwhelm me and I wouldn't be able to go on. Somehow, I found the words. 'But it's alright. I know I'll be okay, even though I'm going to feel very, very sad. When I miss you, I shall think of you on one of your little walks with your new owner and I shall smile, even though my heart will be breaking again.'

Princess looked up at me. Possibly for the last time, her head was cocked to one side, her eyes staring into mine. I kissed her nose and she rewarded me with a giant, drooling kiss, which made me laugh with sheer delight.

'We know you're compatible because your new owner came and took you out by himself to see if you could walk the same sort of distance together in the woods. He's so excited to have you, and I know you'll be happy together.'

Placing the right animal with the right owner was a skill to rival any relationship match maker. The fact that this chap had found us had put me on my guard at first, but after I'd seen the natural affection they had for each other, I was happy to step back from match making for once.

I looked around again. 'Time is marching on, Princess. We'll have a few more goes with the ball then we must head back. I don't want to be accused of kidnapping you out here.' I ruffled her fur, then pulled my arm back and threw the ball with all my might.

'Go, Princess, go!' I shouted, giggling at her funny half run, half walk, my heart swelling with pride for her.

Back at the kennels, I waited with Fran. At the sound of Mr Smith's car tyres crunching on the gravel driveway, my heart swooped down into my belly.

'He's here,' Fran said.

I couldn't speak. I didn't know how to say goodbye to the dog I'd loved back to health and happiness, though we had never been able to get her a false front leg. On that, I felt I had failed, but looking at Princess's happiness, I knew that it was okay after all. She was coping brilliantly without a front leg now that she had perfected her limp.

'I'd better go and welcome him,' I said quietly, and headed out to the gate. Each step brought Princess's departure closer. My head was swimming, and I felt strangely cold and faint.

'Hello,' I managed to say.

Mr Smith looked at me and in his glance, I saw that he understood.

'Good morning, Miss Keel. I'll leave the boot open for Princess to get inside.' He chatted about silly things, which dog bed he'd bought for Princess, how many times he'd take her for a walk each day, and I nodded politely. Part of me wanted this ordeal to be over, the other part of me never wanted it to end because the ending meant saying goodbye for the last time.

'There she is,' the elderly man said as he entered the kennels. 'Ready to go, girl?'

Princess went wild with delight, limping over, her tongue lolling out of her face again. I couldn't help but smile at this genuine feeling between the two.

'She'll be in good hands, I promise,' the elderly chap said, looking back at me meaningfully.

'I know,' I said, my voice cracking.

'Do you want to say goodbye? I think it best if we don't draw out our leaving. Everything's ready for her at home, and I want to get her settled as quickly as possible.'

The old man's eyes twinkled as he spoke. Strangely, they were blue, just like my father's. Why hadn't I noticed that before?

I knelt down next to the boxer, her coat shining, her body fleshed over and sleek. I stroked my hand down her back, then pulled her into a cuddle. I could feel the wetness of my tears on her coat, but I carried on as if I'd never let go.

Fran and Mr Smith had stepped back to give me some space with the dog, which I was grateful for.

'We thought this day would never come,' I said eventually. The soppy great dog licked my nose as if to reply: 'Thank you, you've been a great mummy, but now I have to go.'

Behind me, Fran coughed. My time was up. I could extend the goodbye no longer.

I looked into her beautiful dark eyes for the last time.

'Goodbye, Princess.'

I stood up, tears streaming down my face. Fran's eyes were moist too. Princess had made an impact on so many people here with her courage and spirit.

'Home time for us, girl,' her new owner said.

I walked slowly behind them, both of them limping along, already absorbed in each other's company. I stood at the gate and watched as the gent heaved the boxer up into his car with surprising strength.

'They're going to be fine,' said Fran, who I hadn't realised was standing next to me. My eyes were blurred with tears, watching the impossible happen: Princess had found her forever home. She was off to start her new life with a loving new owner.

At that point, Harry trotted up and put his paw against my leg as if to say: 'I'm still here.' I blinked to clear my sight and smiled down at him. The three of us stayed there, witnessing Princess's departure, until the car had reversed round and driven out of the lane. Harry pawed again, and I realised he needed feeding. It was a reminder that life goes on. I had lost my beloved father. I had said goodbye to a dog I thought would live with me forever, but all I could feel on that sunny, mild spring morning was a sense of joy and peace.

'Come on, you lot, there's work to be done,' I said, wiping away the tears that ran freely down my face. 'We have a sanctuary to run.'

When Do the Elephants Arrive?

Every day, the work of the Barby Keel Animal Sanctuary goes on. Every day, we receive new unwanted animals to find homes for, to feed, wash, treat and love. Ponies and horses outlive their usefulness as riding animals and are often abandoned to make way for younger models. Pigs and sheep are given to us by people who dream of a smallholding (or who saw the film *Babe*), but find the reality overwhelming, time-consuming and more like hard work than a fantasy of farming.

Goats are often left because owners have brought them to graze on their land but find that as well as eating the weeds and nettles, they eat everything else as well, including flowers, vegetables and plants.

Dogs are neglected, beaten, starved and cast out, or simply discarded because they are too energetic for a household.

Cats arrive amid a torrent of excuses, ranging from the owner falling pregnant to children preferring to play with a kitten rather than the full-grown cat they become.

Rabbits, guinea pigs and hamsters are left at our door because children grow tired or bored of them, parents get fed up with feeding them and cleaning them out in the face of their children's lack of interest.

Our peacocks and guinea fowls screeched their way into the sanctuary, after being rehomed due to their persistent, and unappealing, noise-making.

Most of these foster animals could've stayed with their owners if they'd been handled or treated properly, and yet the sanctuary exists because they weren't.

We never judge anyone for handing an animal over to us; not because we are saints – far from it – but because it would put people off coming to us, then unwanted animals might be dumped anywhere and perish if not taken in by an organisation such as ours.

When other small, private sanctuaries shut down, as they do all too often, we take in whatever we can. I will never turn an animal away if I can help it. In fact, the only time I have to is when our kennels are full, as we are allowed only seven dogs on the site at once, following the introduction of a new measure by the council, perhaps as a result of our court case. It was never explained to me, but a condition of our planning permission for the sanctuary would now be limiting our intake to seven dogs at any one time in the kennels.

Injured animals find their way to us via members of the public, who are vigilant and unceasing in their efforts to rescue injured seagulls, birds, pheasants and pigeons. Most of these animals are feral and so, once healed, they are released back into their natural habitat.

And then there are the desperate cases where owners are forced to give up their beloved family pet due to dire financial straits or relocation. Tyrannical landlords are giving tenants an ultimatum: get rid of your pet or lose your home. These cases are particularly heartbreaking, as are the rehomings where someone has been struck down with incurable illness, or gone into a care home.

Our visitors always wonder at the sheer variety of species we care for here. Every Sunday during visiting hours in the spring and summer, curious well-wishers ask me, 'How do you cope?' and I reply stoutly, 'With a lot of help!'

One day, a few years ago, someone came up to me and asked: 'When do the elephants arrive?' I assumed it was a joke because we had pretty much every other species of animal that Noah might've put into the ark!

The reality of our work here is that we survive from day to day. We rely on the kindness of people who know of our sanctuary, and of others who may have heard of the tireless work we all do saving distressed animals from worse suffering.

We rely on people like you, the reader. People who buy my books and who, in doing so, support the ongoing work of our sanctuary in the beautiful Sussex countryside. I can't thank you individually, but my gratitude goes to you all. By reading this, you are helping us to carry on the vital work we do caring for the strays, abandoned and cast-out creatures who find comfort and shelter at my site. Without those souls who donate money, who buy my books or who visit the sanctuary, we wouldn't be able to do any of this. My passion for fostering animals would be unfulfilled, and saving them would be an impossible task.

If you would like to learn more about the sanctuary, or donate money to help our creatures, then please go to our website: https://barbykeel.btck.co.uk/

If you can foster a dog or cat, or even sponsor one if you cannot take an animal into your home, please go to: Dogs at Barby Keel Sanctuary on Facebook.

We can't promise you good breeding, we can't promise an easy ride, but we can promise that you'll know the pleasure of giving an abandoned dog or cat a safe and welcoming home.

Princess's story showed me, if I didn't already know it, that there is always hope, even in the darkest times. She showed me that miracles do happen, dogs that appear to be hopeless cases can find forever homes, even if, sometimes, it takes years rather than days.

The future of the sanctuary looks brighter than it has for a long time. We have money in the bank to carry out essential works. We have caring, devoted staff who put the animals first every single time, and we have the knowledge that our existence alone provides a safe harbour in the desperate raging storms of life.

I have never taken this special place for granted, the wonderful people it contains or the menagerie of happy animals that are in our care. I leave you with our mission: that *any* animal finding their way here is given dignity and love, no matter what.